JN084357

NHK
WORLD
JAPAN

NHK

Tatsuroh Yamazaki
Stella M. Yamazaki

NEWSLINE 7

KINSEIDO

Kinseido Publishing Co., Ltd.

3-21 Kanda Jimbo-cho, Chiyoda-ku,
Tokyo 101-0051, Japan

First published 2024 by Kinseido Publishing Co., Ltd.

Cover design: Takayuki Minegishi
Text design: DAITECH co., ltd.

Video materials NHK (Japan Broadcasting Corporation)

Authors and publisher are grateful to NHK Global Media Services, Inc. and all the interviewees who appeared on the news.

はじめに

　NHK NEWSLINE のテキストシリーズが刊行されてから、本書で 7 冊目を迎えることができた。これも皆さま方のご支援によるもので心より感謝申し上げる。

　地球規模の気候変動が起きている現在、日々の情報から目が離せないが、特に Z 世代（1995 〜 2010 年頃生まれ）やそれ以降の若い人々には不確かな将来が待っている。特に環境問題は待ったなしである。カーボンニュートラルを見据えて、いろいろな努力がなされているが、例えば、航空機の燃料として家庭で廃棄されていた食用油を従来の燃料に混ぜて使用したり、バイオ燃料の利用で CO_2 の排出量を大幅に削減したりしている。大学生や高校生など若い世代がそうした問題に積極的に取り組んでいる姿は、これからのリーダーたちとして大いに頼もしい限りである。

　さらに身近な国際問題としては、輸出入制限や物価高騰などの政治的・経済的課題があるが、関税をなくして経済活動を推進しようという TPP（環太平洋経済連携協定）やグローバル・サウスとの話し合いなど枚挙にいとまがない。こうした国々の人たちと直接話すときやプレゼンの共通言語は英語である。英語での会話力をつけるのはもはや、国際交流では前提としなければいけない。

　会話は音声のインプットとアウトプットの合わせ技だが、外国語は徹底的に聞いて模倣するという姿勢が常に必要である。従って伝統的な反復練習や文型練習は、語学学習者にとって必修である。目で追うだけではなく何回か反復して「音読」しておこう。音読しておけば記憶に定着しやすく、会話でもとっさの時に出てくるという利点がある。学習者にとって外国語の会話は（運動競技と同様に）スキルであり、練習によって積み上げた「記憶」が頼りなのである。

　本書はリスニングを中心課題に据えたニュースの視聴覚教材である。ニュースは NHK 海外向け放送の *NEWSLINE* から採択し、適切な長さに編集した。この番組は現代日本の主な出来事や経済、文化、科学の最近の動向などを簡潔にまとめており好評を博している。

　語学は授業中の学習だけではじゅうぶんではない。現在、ニュース映像がオンラインで視聴可能となった。自宅で納得するまで繰り返し見てほしい。その際、まず完成したスクリプト（News Story の穴埋め問題終了後）を見ながら音声と意味の対応を頭に入れ、その後は文字を見ないで聞くという作業が必要である。この繰り返しが何回かあれば、文字なしで映像音声の理解ができるという快感が味わえるようになる。

　末筆ながら、本書の作成に関して金星堂編集部をはじめ関係スタッフの方々に大変お世話になった。更に出版にあたって NHK、株式会社 NHK グローバルメディアサービスの皆様にも映像提供などでご協力をいただいた。ここに厚くお礼を申し上げる。

2024 年 1 月　　　　　　　　　　　　　　編著者：山﨑達朗／ Stella M. Yamazaki

本書の構成とねらい

本書は全部で 15 単元（units）からなり、各単元とも、① 日本語のイントロダクション、② Words & Phrases、③ Before You Watch、④ Watch the News、⑤ Understand the News、⑥ Listen to the News Story、⑦ Review the Key Expressions、⑧ Discussion Questions という構成になっている。このうち①と②は説明で、③〜⑧が練習問題である。

① 日本語のイントロダクション

この短い日本語の説明は、ニュースの要点を把握することを目的としている。外国語のリスニングには、何がどのように飛び出してくるかわからないという緊張と不安が常に伴うので、このように限られた背景知識（background knowledge）でも、予め準備があると安心感が出るものである。

② Words & Phrases

比較的難しいか、カギになる語彙や熟語などを学習する。ここで意味的、文法的知識をつけておけば、ニュースを聞いた場合に戸惑いは少なくなる。必要に応じて簡単な例文も入れてある。

③ Before You Watch

ニュース映像を見る前に、その予備知識を獲得したり話題を膨らませたりする意味で単元ごとに違った課題が用意してある。内容的には、日常会話表現の学習であったり、社会・文化に特有な語彙を英語でどう言うかといった課題であったりする。また通じにくい和製英語の表現に触れたり、語源の重要性に特化したものもある。

④ Watch the News — 1st Viewing

ここで初めてクラスで映像を見るわけだが、課題はニュース内容の大きな流れや要点の理解が主となる基本的把握である。設問が3つあり、各問とも内容に合っていれば T（= True）、合っていなければ F（= False）を選択し、問題文の真偽を判断する。外国語のリスニングはしぜんに耳から入ってくるということがないので、集中して聞く必要がある。必要に応じて随時、視聴の回数を増やしたり、問題と関連する箇所を教師が集中的に見せたりするということが過去の経験から有効である。

⑤ Understand the News — 2nd Viewing

同じニュース映像をもう一度見るが、内容についてやや詳細な質問となっている。次の2種類の下位区分がある。ここも必要に応じ、複数回のリスニングを考慮していただきたい。

1 最初の視聴と比べて今度は選択肢が3つになっており、内容もより詳細にわたる設問が用意してある。各問、左端の3枚の写真は、参考にはなるが、問題を解く上でリスニングのキーとなる部分の映像とは限らないので注意してほしい。

2 単元によって、何種類か様々な形式の設問が用意してある。いずれもニュース内容の確認を目的としている。例えばニュースのまとめとなる「概要」や「事柄の時系列的な順序づけ」、要点となる数字の記入などである。さらに、設問によっては、ややゲーム的な要素を考慮し、アルファベットの並べ替え（unscrambling）を入れている。

⑥ Listen to the News Story

これはニュース映像に対応するスクリプトであるが、完全なものにするには「穴埋め問題」を解く必要がある。問題は合計7問で、各問題に6〜8か所の空所がある。解答するには，スタジオでややゆっくり読まれた音声CDをクラスで（各2回繰り返し）聞きながら書き取り作業（dictation）をする。スクリプトのそれぞれの問題には、右端におおよその日本語訳が付けてあるのでヒントになる。書き取りが完成すればニュース映像の全文が目で確かめられるが、スクリプトは映像を見る前に読むことはせず、まず何回か視聴して上記④と⑤の設問に解答した後に、この穴埋めに挑戦してほしい。

⑦ Review the Key Expressions

ここでは、映像で出てきた単語や熟語などのうち応用性のある表現に習熟することがねらいである。そのような重要表現の意味や用法を確実にするとともに、英作文があまり負担なく身につくように単語を与える「整序問題」形式（4問）を採用した。ただし選択肢の中に錯乱肢（distractors）を1語入れ、適度に難しくしてある。文例は当該単元の話題とは関係なく、いろいろな場面の設定になっている。

⑧ Discussion Questions

最後の問題として、クラス内での話し合いに使える話題を2つ用意してある。当該単元に関連した身近な話題が提示してあるので、短く簡単な英語で自分の考えを表現してみる、というのがねらいである。（ご指導の先生方へ：クラスによっては宿題として、話すことを次回までに考えておくというスタンスや自由英作文としてもよいと思われる。この話し合いの課題は、人数や時間などクラス設定との兼ね合いから、用途に応じて柔軟に扱うのがよいと考えられる。）

NHK NEWSLINE 7

CONTENTS

UNIT 01

Studying in the Metaverse

メタバース学習塾

メタバースはインターネット上の仮想空間自体や、そこで行うコミュニケーションのサービス・プロダクト全般を指すが、その空間では分身のアバターを自由に操作することができる。この予備校では、VRゴーグルなどの特別な機器ではなく、パソコンのみを使用して授業を受けたり人と交流したりでき、今後の教育に大きな影響をもたらすと期待されている。

放送日 2022/9/29

Words & Phrases

◉ CD 02

以下の単語や熟語の音声を聞きながら発音に注意し、意味を確認しましょう。

☐ **metaverse**　　メタバース

☐ **cram school**　　予備校、進学塾

☐ **avatar**　　アバター

☐ to **represent**　　～を表す、の代わりになる

☐ to **socialize**　　交流する、おしゃべりする

例文 Tsuyoshi seems to spend all his time *socializing*.
剛は自分の時間すべてを人との付き合いに使っているようだ。

☐ **technical**　　機械の

☐ **specifications**　　スペック〈製品やサービスの仕様や性能を表す〉

例文 The *specifications* [specs] show that this computer is not capable of using the latest game software.
このコンピューターのスペックでは、その最新ゲームソフトは動かない。

☐ **frozen**　　フリーズした、（画像が）静止した

以下は、英語の授業で使う表現です。下の枠内から適切な単語を選び、空所に入れましょう。

1. Let me take (　　　　　　　　). 　　　出席をとります。

2. *Teacher:* Tim Conway? 　　　　　　ティム・コンウェイ君(はいますか)。
   Tim: (　　　　　　　　). 　　　　はい(ここにいます)。

3. Please (　　　　　　　) to page 32 in your textbooks.
   　　　　　　　　　　　　　　　　　教科書32ページを開いてください。

4. Could you (　　　　　　) that again? 　もう一度言ってください。

5. Are you (　　　　　　) me? 　　　　私の説明がわかりますか。

6. Any (　　　　　　)? 　　　　　　誰かやってくれますか。

7. (　　　　　　) up to the (　　　　　　) and write your answer on the board.
   　　　　　　　　　　　　　　　　　前に出て黒板に答えを書いてください。

8. (　　　　　　) your hand if you have any questions.
   　　　　　　　　　　　　　　　　　質問があれば手を上げてください。

9. Please read this sentence (　　　　　　). この文を音読してください。

10. (　　　　　　) after me. 　　　　私の後に続いて読んでください。

11. Please work with the person (　　　　　) to you.
    　　　　　　　　　　　　　　　　隣の人と一緒にやってください。

12. Let me give you this week's (　　　　　). 今週の課題を出します。

13. It's (　　　　　　) next Monday. 　締め切りは来週の月曜日です。

14. We don't have (　　　　　) time (　　　　　).
    　　　　　　　　　　　　　　　　残り時間があまりありません。

15. That's (　　　　　　) for today. 　今日はこれで終わりです。

| all | aloud | assignment | attendance | come | due | front | here |
| left | much | next | raise | repeat | say | turn | volunteers | with |

ニュースを見て、内容と合っているものは T 、違っているものは F を選びましょう。

1. The popularity of online learning has little to do with the pandemic. 　T・F

2. The principal of this school realized that students became more active in virtual classes. 　T・F

3. The cram school hosted an event to promote the school. 　T・F

2

2nd Viewing ≫ Understand the News

1 ニュースをもう一度見て、各問の空所に入る適切な選択肢を a ~ c から選びましょう。

1. Students make a line in front of the _____.

   a. socializing area
   b. gym entrance
   c. question room

2. During the school event, there were _____.

   a. too many people
   b. network-related problems
   c. some complicated questions

Kikuta Keita
Teacher, Kai Seminar

3. _____ of the people who attended the event couldn't enter cyberspace.

   a. One third
   b. One half
   c. Two thirds

2 右の文字列を並べ替えて単語を作り、各文の空所に入れて意味がとおるようにしましょう。語頭の文字（群）が与えてあるものもあります。

1. These students participate from home in virtual classes as (　　　　　)《複数形》.
   [traaavs]

2. There is a virtual space where students can (**so**　　　　) with each other.
   [clazeii]

3. The principal sees a (**po**　　　　) change in the students' attitudes. [tisvei]

4. The screen (**f**　　　　) when there was a technical problem in the virtual lesson.
   [zero]

Listen to the News Story

CDの音声を聞いて、News Story の ❶～❼ の文中にある空所に適切な単語を書き入れましょう。音声は２回繰り返されます。

Anchor: Online learning has become a business opportunity in the pandemic. One **cram school** in Japan has taken advantage of the situation to improve its services, enabling students to attend as **avatars** from home. We have more from NHK World's Kohmoto Kyohta.

Narrator: This is a cram school in Yamanashi Prefecture. Last year, it began using the metaverse to offer virtual classes to third-year junior high school students. The characters sitting in front of the classroom chalkboard are avatars, **representing** each of the *student*[s].

  ❶ I also created an avatar (¹) (²) (³) (⁴) (⁵) (⁶). Walking around outside the classrooms, there are spaces designed for relaxation. This is where students can take a break and **socialize**.

Girl student: My classmates' avatars are here, too. ❷ I like the metaverse (¹) (²) (³) (⁴) (⁵) (⁶).

Narrator: Metaverse classes offer unique experiences. In math class, for example, the teachers spin some of the shapes to illustrate a point.

  Surprisingly, students are also lining up in front of the question room.

Teacher (Avatar): Nice to meet you.

Boy student: ❸ I'm very shy and (¹) (²) (³) (⁴) (⁵) (⁶) in front of others. It's easier in the metaverse.

Narrator: School principal Osada Masaki was behind the idea of virtual

❶ この学校 (内) を歩き回れるように

❷ ここで楽しめるからです

❸ 質問するのが難しい

classes and has seen a positive shift in the attitudes of the students.

Osada Masaki *(Principal, Kai Seminar):* The students' ability to concentrate has changed completely, and they speak up here, unlike in real classes.

Narrator: The cram school held an event in July to attract more students. ❹ Students (¹) (²) (³) (⁴) (⁵) (⁶) (⁷). ❺ (¹) (²) (³) (⁴) (⁵) (⁶).

❹ 全国から招待された

❺ いろいろな地域から、大体〜人が応募した

The event was a success, but there were some **technical** issues. Some students couldn't enter cyberspace because their computers didn't have the required **specifications**.

Kikuta Keita *(Teacher, Kai Seminar):* There's no sound, and the video is **frozen**.

Narrator: About two thirds of those attending couldn't participate. But Osada is hopeful. ❻ This technology will (¹) (²) (³) (⁴) (⁵) (⁶).

❻ 教育において必須の道具になる

Osada: The metaverse will probably be commonplace in a few years. ❼ I want to (¹) (²) (³) (⁴) (⁵) (⁶) to adapt to the future.

❼ 仮想空間でクラスを作る

Narrator: The metaverse is already attracting attention in many fields. It may now be time for the education sector to **take its place** in the virtual spotlight. Kohmoto Kyohta, NHK World, Kofu.

Note: 使用画面は2022年当時のもの。現在は違ったインターフェイスになっている。

（p. 4）ℓ. 10 *student* は、複数形 students が正しい

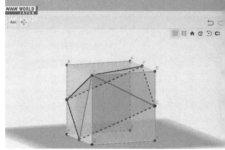

各問、選択肢から適切な単語を選び、英文を完成させましょう。なお、余分な単語が 1 語ずつあります。

1. 梅雨の時期のあいだ、めったにない今日のような良い天候を<u>利用して</u>外出すべきだ。

    (　　　　　　) the (　　　　　　) (　　　　　　　　), we should (＿＿＿＿＿＿＿)
    (＿＿＿＿＿＿＿) of rare, sunny days (　　　　　　) today for (　　　　　　).

season	rainy	outings	advantage	like	take	during	meanwhile

2. 仕事で集中力を維持するために、従業員たちは規則的に<u>休憩をとる</u>べきだ。

    To (　　　　　　) (　　　　　　) on the (　　　　　　), (　　　　　　) should
    (＿＿＿＿＿＿) regular (＿＿＿＿＿＿).

breaks	maintain	employees	job	take	concentration	employers

3. 多くの人は、新しいゲーム機を買うのに、何時間も<u>列を作って</u>待つのを気にしないようだ。

    Many people (　　　　　　) (　　　　　　) to (　　　　　　) (＿＿＿＿＿＿) up
    and (　　　　　　) for (　　　　　　) to (　　　　　　) new game machines.

waiting	feel	buy	mind	hours	lining	don't	seem

4. グレタ・トゥーンベリは、いつも環境保護に関するスピーチで<u>関心を引く</u>。

    Greta Thunberg (　　　　　　) (＿＿＿＿＿＿) (　　　　　　) with her
    (　　　　　　) on (　　　　　　) the (　　　　　　).

attention	environment	speeches	always	attracts	global	protecting

1. If you were studying for college entrance exams, would you prefer to take regular classes or metaverse classes? Why?

2. Name one thing that has greatly improved your life since junior high school. Explain.

6

UNIT 02

Japanese Firms Switching to English Amid Engineer Shortage

人材不足で英語公用語

APANESE IT FIRMS SWITCHING TO ENGLISH AMID ENGINEER SHORTAGE

海外ではITエンジニアを見つけるのはそれほど難しくないが、日本ではそうした技術者が大きく不足している。それを解決するカギとなるのが英語コミュニケーション能力である。日本の大手の会社では「公用語」が英語となり、その傾向は拡大すると見込まれる。今後の国際競争で必須となる英語能力の最前線を追ってみた。

放送日 2022/11/28

Words & Phrases

CD 04

以下の単語や熟語の音声を聞きながら発音に注意し、意味を確認しましょう。

- ☐ **start-up** 新興企業
- ☐ **warehouse** 卸売店、倉庫
- ☐ **artificial intelligence** 人工知能
- ☐ **workforce** 従業員、労働力
- ☐ **human resources** 人的資源
- ☐ **domestic** 国内の

例文 We should buy more *domestic* products.
私たちは国内産の商品をもっと買うべきだ。

- ☐ **staff** [stæf]〈発音に注意〉 スタッフ、従業員
- ☐ **crucial** 極めて重要な、決定的な

例文 Winning the contract this year is *crucial* to the success of our company.
今年その契約をとることが、私たちの会社が成功するのに絶対必要だ。

- ☐ **mindset** ものの考え方
- ☐ **office hours** 仕事時間、営業時間

以下は略語に関する問題です。1〜12の空所に当てはまる英語を下のアルファベット表から見つけ、線で囲みましょう。囲み方は縦、横、斜めいずれも可能です。

例 AI（　　**Artificial**　　）Intelligence　　　　　　人工知能

1. CEO（　　　　　　　）Executive Officer　　　　最高経営責任者

2. VIP（　　　　　　　）Important Person　　　　　要人

3. ATM Automated（　　　　　　　）Machine　　現金自動預け払い機

4. FAQ Frequently（　　　　　　　）Questions　　よくある質問

5. DIY（　　　　　　）It Yourself　　　　　　　日曜大工、素人仕事

6. UFO Unidentified Flying（　　　　　　）　　未確認飛行物体

7. IMO In My（　　　　　　）　　　　　　　　私の意見では

8. BTW By The（　　　　　）　　　　　　　　ところで

9. ASAP As Soon As（　　　　　　）　　　　　できるだけ早く

10. FYI For Your（　　　　　）　　　　　　　ご参考まで

11. TGIF Thank（　　　　　）It's Friday　　　ヤッター、金曜日だ！

12. TOEFL Test of English as a（　　　　　　　）Language

外国語としての英語テスト（TOEFL）

	1	2	3	4	5	6	7	8	9	10	11	12	13	14	15	16
A	F	U	N	G	V	A	S	E	F	Z	Q	W	O	A	C	T
B	I	N	F	O	R	M	A	T	I	O	N	A	P	D	D	O
C	G	O	L	D	S	P	O	I	N	T	R	Y	I	D	E	B
D	A	S	K	E	D	V	O	I	C	E	P	E	N	K	T	J
E	D	E	C	H	I	E	F	D	P	O	S	S	I	B	L	E
F	V	E	R	Y	A	T	E	L	L	E	R	T	O	G	S	C
G	A	R	T	I	F	I	C	I	A	L	W	A	N	D	N	T

1st Viewing ≫ **Watch the News**

ニュースを見て、内容と合っているものは T、違っているものは F を選びましょう。

1. The employees communicate in English except in cases where all group members understand Japanese.　　　　　　　　T・F

2. Komaki is happy to employ AI specialists from all over the world.　　T・F

3. Komaki says that his company's ultimate goal is to become successful in AI.　T・F

2nd Viewing 》》 **Understand the News**

1 ニュースをもう一度見て、各問の空所に入る適切な選択肢を a ~ c から選びましょう。

Tadokoro Saori
Talent Acquisition Partner, Rapyuta Robotics

1. In this Japanese company, _____.

   a. all employees are foreign nationals
   b. less than 20 percent of the engineers are non-Japanese
   c. over 80 percent of the engineers are foreigners

Komaki Masakazu
Manager, Global Division, Money Forward

2. According to Komaki, _____.

   a. it is hard to employ Japanese AI engineers
   b. most AI engineers speak English
   c. English is not the official language at his company

3. According to Komaki's company rules, _____.

   a. at least one member of the small units has to be a non-Japanese
   b. fewer than half of the small unit members must be Japanese
   c. not more than a quarter of the small unit members are Japanese

2 右の文字列を並べ替えて単語を作り、各文の空所に入れて意味がとおるようにしましょう。語頭の文字（群）は与えてあります。

1. In some Japanese companies, (**E**   ) is used as the official language.
   [lgnhis]

2. Komaki says that his company's (**f**   ) goal is to become a tech giant.
   [nlai]

3. A business or company can also be called a (**f**   ).   [mri]

4. A person who is paid to work is called an (**em**   ).   [leepoy]

CDの音声を聞いて、News Story の ❶〜❼ の文中にある空所に適切な単語を書き入れましょう。音声は2回繰り返されます。

Narrator: This **start-up** in Tokyo develops **warehouse** robots that use **artificial intelligence**. More than 80 percent of the firm's engineers are non-Japanese. A steady stream of overseas recruits is being added to the company's **workforce**. Despite being a Japanese company, most communication is in English.

5

Tadokoro Saori (Talent Acquisition Partner, Rapyuta Robotics): Our company eliminates barriers between Japanese and foreigners, and recruits with the stance that we want excellent **human resources**, regardless of nationality.

10

Yasui Seiichi (NHK World): ❶ Companies like this used to (1)
(2) (3) (4)
(5) (6) (7),
but now it's **domestic staff** who need to speak English.

❶ 外国の社員に流ちょうな日本語を話すことを要求する

15 *Narrator:* Tokyo-based tech firm, Money Forward is tackling the challenge. English was adopted a year ago as the official internal language. A company official says bringing in foreign talent is **crucial** to meet global competition.

Komaki Masakazu (Manager, Global Division, Money Forward): ❷ In Japan,
20 (1) (2) (3)
(4) (5) (6)
(7) because the number of AI engineers is very limited in Japan. But [the] situation is different overseas. Outside of Japan, we can find easily AI engineers.

❷ AI技術者を雇うのは難しすぎる

25 *Narrator:* ❸ A human resource expert says (1)
(2) (3) (4)
(5) (6) (7)
for Japanese business people.

❸ 英語はますます必須になってきている

Ando Masuyo (Chairman of the Board, Progos): They have to realize that they are losing a lot of opportunities for career expansion and business opportunities, because of the lack of [the] English skills.

30

So, they have to change their **mindset** and jump into the English-speaking business world.

Narrator: ❹ (¹) (²) (³)
(⁴) (⁵) (⁶).

❹ 英語への切換えは簡単ではない

5　To ease the transition, Money Forward has made English the official language within this small unit.

The company requires that no more than 25 percent of the team members be Japanese. ❺ The aim is to put them in

❺ 英語を話さなければならない環境

(¹) (²) (³)
10　(⁴) (⁵) (⁶)
(⁷). Some are struggling, but it's good training.

Doran The Long (Money Forward): I cannot express myself much in Japanese, so it's a good opportunity to *know*[*1] my *coworker*[*s*][*2] better, and
15　I can express myself better in English.

Narrator: ❻ Employees (¹) (²)
(³) (⁴) (⁵)
(⁶) (⁷).

❻ 仕事時間中に英語を勉強することができる

(*Cellphone recording*)

20　*Phone:* The news made her excited.

Employee: (*She repeats*) The news made her excited. ❼ Did
(¹) (²) (³)
(⁴) (⁵) (⁶)
(⁷)?

❼ 彼は夜遅く帰宅しまし(たか)

25　*Narrator:* Komaki says welcoming AI talent from around the world and adopting English will help *toward* product development and expand business.

Komaki: I think we can become...we can get the opportunity to become one of the tech *giant*[*s*]. That's our final goal.

30　*Narrator:* The huge demand for engineers has the potential to dramatically change the business environment for both foreign and domestic tech workers in Japan. Yasui Seiichi, NHK World.

Notes: (p. 10) ℓ. 31　このtheは文法的に不要　(p. 11) ℓ. 14　*1 get to knowのほうがしぜん
*2 複数形がしぜん　ℓ. 26　withのほうがしぜん　ℓ. 29　giantsが正しい

Review the Key Expressions

各問、選択肢から適切な単語を選び、英文を完成させましょう。なお、余分な単語が1語ずつあります。

1. その子どもたちは天候にかかわらず、日曜日に外でサッカーの練習をすると決めた。

   The (　　　　　) (　　　　　) to (　　　　　) out and (　　　　　)
   soccer on Sunday (＿＿＿＿＿) (＿＿＿＿＿) the (　　　　　).

of	decided	regardless	go	weather	although	kids	practice

2. 彼はかなり成功した多くの起業家と同じ考え方だ。

   He (　　　　　) the (　　　　　) (＿＿＿＿＿) (　　　　　) many
   (　　　　　) successful (　　　　　).

as	same	mindset	entrepreneurs	soon	highly	has

3. 私の昼寝の時間はふつう30分を超えない。

   I (　　　　　) limit (　　　　　) to (＿＿＿＿＿) (＿＿＿＿＿)
   (＿＿＿＿＿) half an (　　　　　).

hour	usually	than	more	less	naps	no

4. 多くの恥ずかしがりやの人たちは、話すよりも書くことで自分をよりうまく表現できる。

   Many (　　　　　) people can (＿＿＿＿＿) (＿＿＿＿＿) (　　　　　)
   in (　　　　　) than by (　　　　　).

speaking	talkative	shy	better	writing	themselves	express

Discussion Questions

1. Would you like to work at a company where English is used as the official language? Why or why not? Explain.

2. Which is the most difficult English skill for you: speaking, listening, reading or writing? Explain.

12

Recycling Car Parts Into Fashion Treasure

UNIT 03

エアバッグが洋服に

RECYCLING CAR PARTS INTO FASHION TREASURE

未使用のまま廃品となっていた自動車のエアバッグを有効活用するSDGsへの取り組みが注目されている。山陰の大手企業が国際的なデザイナーと協力して洋服に生まれ変わらせたのである。いわゆる「アップサイクル」という活動だが、その作品の展示会がこのほど行われ、受注生産での全国販売を始める運びとなった。

放送日 2022/1/12

Words & Phrases

◎ CD 06

以下の単語や熟語の音声を聞きながら発音に注意し、意味を確認しましょう。

- ☐ **million**　　　　100万
- ☐ **vehicle**　　　　〈車などの〉乗り物
  - 例文 After the head-on collision, the *vehicle* was totally destroyed.
    正面衝突後、その車は完全に壊れた。
- ☐ to **end up**　　　（結局）〜に終わる
- ☐ **component**　　　〈車などの〉部品、部分
- ☐ to **figure out**　　答えを出す、理解する
- ☐ **fiber**　　　　　（1本の）繊維
- ☐ **durability**　　　耐久性、持続力
- ☐ **intact**　　　　　損なわれていない、無傷の
- ☐ **fabric**　　　　　繊維
- ☐ to **try on**　　　　試着する
  - 例文 Can I *try* this shirt *on* in a fitting room?
    このシャツを試着室で着てみていいですか。

以下は、車や交通などに関する表現です。下の枠内から適切な単語を選び、空所に入れましょう。なお、余分な語彙もあります。

1. 彼は酒酔い運転で逮捕された。　He was arrested for (　　　　　　　) driving.

2. 小石を満載したダンプカーがスリップして道路からそれた。
   A (　　　　　　　) (　　　　　　　) with a full load of gravel skidded off the road.

3. 一番近くのガソリンスタンドはどこですか。
   Where is the closest (　　　　　　　) (　　　　　　　)?

4. 兄[弟]のオープンカーは、屋根を下ろして運転すると楽しい。
   My brother's (　　　　　　　) is fun to drive with the top down.

5. 何か硬いものが車のフロントガラスにあたった。
   Something hard hit the (　　　　　　　) of my car.

6. ウインカーが壊れているようだ。　My (　　　　　　　) don't seem to be working.

7. 中古車展示場には車がぎっしりと置かれた。
   The cars were parked (　　　　　　　) to bumper in the used car (　　　　　　　).

8. 東京にはバスや電車などいろいろな公共交通機関がある。
   In Tokyo there are various forms of (　　　　　　　) (　　　　　　　) such as
   buses and trains.

9. 通勤の途中車が壊れて、レッカー車を呼ばなければいけなかった。
   My car broke down on the way to work and I had to call a (　　　　　　　) truck.

10. 車がパンクした。　My car has a (　　　　　　　) tire.

blinkers	brake	bumper	convertible	drunk	dump	flat
freeway	gas	jaywalking	lot	public	rearview	station
tow	transportation	truck	wheel	windshield		

ニュースを見て、内容と合っているものは T 、違っているものは F を選びましょう。

1. Over three billion cars are recycled in Japan every year.　　T・F

2. This airbag recycling project started in Tottori Prefecture.　　T・F

3. A recycling specialist says that airbags are strong and stay in good condition for a
   long time.　　T・F

1 ニュースをもう一度見て、各問の空所に入る適切な選択肢を a ~ c から選びましょう。

1. This fashion designer made the clothes using _____.

    a. mostly polyester

    b. a blend of cotton and silk

    c. only nylon

2. _____ car parts can be recycled.

    a. Only a small number of

    b. Mainly metal

    c. Almost all

3. The designer produced _____.

    a. just a few items like jackets and pants

    b. nine items, such as hats and bags

    c. over a hundred items, including raincoats

2 以下はニュースの概要です。空所に適切な単語を書き入れましょう。語頭の文字（群）は与えてあります。

An automobile recycling firm in western Japan teamed up with a (**fa** [1]) designer and created clothing items from (**a** [2])《複数形》. (**N** [3]) percent of all auto parts can be recycled, but only this car part has been thrown away up to now. With a lot of effort, the team came up with products, such as hats and (**ja** [4])《複数形》, for display and sale. The (**lo** [5]) store seems to have become popular because of those recycled products. The designer and the recycler feel that they successfully changed waste into (**tr** [6]).

Listen to the News Story

CDの音声を聞いて、News Story の ❶〜❼ の文中にある空所に適切な単語を書き入れましょう。音声は2回繰り返されます。

Anchor: More than three **million vehicles** are recycled annually in Japan. Almost everything finds another use, but one part **ends up** as waste. NHK World's Honda Mina looks at a project aiming to give new life to a key **component** of every car.

Narrator: There is an unusual fashion shoot happening at this automotive recycling plant. ❶ The (　　　　　¹) (　　　　　²) (　　　　　³) (　　　　　⁴) (　　　　　⁵) (　　　　　⁶) (　　　　　⁷), like the ones around him.

> ❶ モデルは車両からリサイクルした洋服を着ている

The clothes are made from a standard item found inside each vehicle, the airbag. This fashion designer has made them entirely out of its material.

Kawanishi Ryohei (Designer): ❷ (　　　　　¹) (　　　　　²) (　　　　　³) (　　　　　⁴) (　　　　　⁵) (　　　　　⁶) (　　　　　⁷) to **figure out** what creative works can do in response to existing problems.

> ❷ 私はそれを実験的な企画とみなしている

Narrator: Ninety-nine percent of the parts in all *vehicle*[s] can be recycled, but airbags are an exception. The nylon **fiber** is not reused. Almost every airbag ends up as waste. This recycler in Tottori Prefecture decided to team up with the local designer to change that.

Nishikawa Tomohiro (Automotive recycling company executive): Airbags have excellent strength and **durability**. If the vehicle has never been involved in an accident, airbags removed from the car will be **intact**, and it would be such a waste to just throw them away.

Narrator: The process takes more time than usual for making *cloth*. ❸ (　　　　　¹) (　　　　　²) (　　　　　³) (　　　　　⁴) (　　　　　⁵) (　　　　　⁶) can be taken from one airbag. Parts cut from several airbags

> ❸ ほんのわずかな量の繊維が…

have to be combined to make a single piece of **fabric**.

Kawanishi: Establishing ways to produce clothes in greater numbers and commercialize them was really challenging. But I'm fully satisfied with what we've created.

Narrator: The designer produced nine items. Serial numbers from the airbags became part of the design.

Kawanishi: ❹ I'm sure (¹) (²) (³) (⁴) (⁵) (⁶) (⁷) (⁸).

❹ 多くの人々が毎日車を運転する

I want people to see how car parts can be turned into what they wear.

Narrator: ❺ (¹) (²) (³) (⁴) (⁵) (⁶) (⁷) at this local store. As soon as it opened,

❺ そのファッション品が12月に飾られた

people crowded in to **try** them **on**. The hats, bags, and jackets were a hit.

Man: I think I'll order one for myself. ❻ The (¹) (²) (³) (⁴) (⁵) (⁶) (⁷).

❻ シリアルナンバーがついているデザインはかっこいい

Narrator: ❼ The designer and the recycler plan to keep working together, (¹) (²) (³) (⁴) (⁵) (⁶) and **turning** what used to be trash **into** treasure. Honda Mina, NHK World, Tottori.

❼ エアバッグをリサイクルする新しい方法を模索しながら

Notes: (p. 16) ℓ. 18　複数形の -sの部分が聞き取りにくい
　　　　　 ℓ. 28　発音が明瞭ではないがcloth が妥当

Reporting
Honda Mina
NHK WORLD

Review the Key Expressions

各問、選択肢から適切な単語を選び、英文を完成させましょう。なお、余分な単語が1語ずつあります。

1. 私たちのアパートは古い雑誌や新聞でいっぱいだ。いつ廃棄するの。

   Our apartment (　　　　　　) (　　　　　　) (　　　　　　) old (　　　　　　)
   and newspapers. When are you going to (＿＿＿＿＿＿) (　　　　　　)
   (＿＿＿＿＿＿)?

full	away	is	throw	of	them	from	magazines

2. 新しいヘッドセットに完全に満足していないなら、返金を依頼することができる。

   If you (　　　　　) (　　　　　　) completely (＿＿＿＿＿) (＿＿＿＿＿)
   the new headset, you can (　　　　　) (　　　　　) your (　　　　　)
   back.

answer	ask	are	money	with	not	for	satisfied

3. できるだけ早く予定をお知らせください。そうすればホテルの予約ができるので。

   Please (　　　　　) us (　　　　　　) your schedule (＿＿＿＿＿)
   (＿＿＿＿＿) (＿＿＿＿＿) you can, so that we can (　　　　　) hotel
   (　　　　　).

as	reservations	soon	visit	let	make	know	as

4. こ（れら）の靴は自分にちょうどいい大きさかな。ためしに履いてみていいですか。

   I'm (　　　　　) (　　　　　　) these shoes (　　　　　) the (　　　　　)
   (　　　　　) for me. Can I (＿＿＿＿＿) them (＿＿＿＿＿)?

on	are	size	wondering	in	right	try	if

Discussion Questions

1. Which would you prefer, driving or taking public transportation? Why?

2. What do you do or are you planning to do to help achieve SDGs (Sustainable Development Goals)?

UNIT 04

Japanese Family Steps Up to Support Evacuee

ウクライナ避難者に寄り添う

Cheers!

PANESE FAMILY STEPS UP TO SUPPORT EVACUEE

ロシアによる軍事侵攻が続く中、ウクライナ人のレナさんが日本に避難してきた。富岡市の佐藤裕さん夫妻らの献身的な努力で、知識ゼロからの日本の生活が始まった。精神的に傷を負った彼女は、クリアすべき生活の課題も多く、家族のことも心配だ。救いは彼女が若いだけに順応性も高く、人への感謝も忘れないところである。

放送日 2022/5/16

Words & Phrases

CD 08

以下の単語や熟語の音声を聞きながら発音に注意し、意味を確認しましょう。

- □ evacuee 避難者
- □ to flee 避難する〈fled は flee の過去・過去分詞形〉
- □ to step up 手を貸す、進み出る
- □ barrage 集中砲火
- □ debris がれき
- □ refugee 難民
- □ to deal with ～に対処する
- □ trauma トラウマ、心的外傷

例文 The cause of his depression is emotional *trauma*.
彼のうつ状態の原因は心的外傷である。

- □ to make sure ～を確かめる、確実に～する

例文 *Make sure* that you lock the door behind you.
出かけるとき、(後ろの)ドアに鍵をかけたかどうか確かめてください。

- □ cheers 《口語》乾杯！

Before You Watch

以下は、生活で必要な身近な品物に関する語彙です。下の枠内から適切な単語を選び、空所に入れましょう。

1. (主に家庭用)トイレ / (主に公共用)トイレ　(　　　　　　　) / (　　　　　　　　) room

2. (紙くず用)ゴミ箱 / (生ごみ用)ゴミ箱　　(　　　　　　　) can / (　　　　　　) can

3. 可燃物 / 不燃物　　　　　　　　　　(　　　　　　　) / (　　　　　　)

4. コンセント　　　　　　　　　　　(　　　　　　　)

5. 携帯電話　　　　　　　　　　　　(　　　　　　　)

6. 充電器　　　　　　　　　　　　　(　　　　　　　)

7. 折り畳み傘　　　　　　　　　　　(　　　　　　　) umbrella

8. 掛け布団　　　　　　　　　　　　(　　　　　　　)

9. 電気コンロ　　　　　　　　　　　electric (　　　　　　　　)

10. 換気扇　　　　　　　　　　　　(　　　　　　　) fan

11. オーブントースター　　　　　　(　　　　　　　) oven

12. ガムテープ　　　　　　　　　　(　　　　　　　) tape

13. セロテープ　　　　　　　　　　(　　　　　　　) tape

14. シャーペン　　　　　　　　　　(　　　　　　　) pencil / (　　　　　　) pencil

15. ビニール袋　　　　　　　　　　(　　　　　　　) bag

automatic	bathroom	burnable	cellphone	charger	folding
garbage	mechanical	nonburnable	outlet	packing	plastic
quilt	rest	Scotch	stove	toaster	trash	ventilating

1st Viewing >> ## Watch the News

ニュースを見て、内容と合っているものは T 、違っているものは F を選びましょう。

1. Lena usually gets help from someone who speaks Ukrainian and Japanese. ☐ T・F

2. Lena reacts negatively to the sound of airplanes because of her traumatic experiences. ☐ T・F

3. In Ukraine, they use cash less often than in Japan. ☐ T・F

1 ニュースをもう一度見て、各問の空所に入る適切な選択肢を a ~ c から選びましょう。

1. Lena traveled from Ukraine to Gunma with _____.

   a. all of her family

   b. only her mother

   c. no family at all

2. Lena is interested in Japanese _____.

   a. animation

   b. theme parks

   c. sports events

3. To help Lena keep active, her host family took her to _____.

   a. an aquarium

   b. a museum

   c. a zoo

2 以下はニュースの概要です。空所に適切な単語を書き入れましょう。語頭の文字（群）は与えてあります。

Hundreds of people fled from (**U**   [1]) to Japan, including Lena Berezhnaya, 21 years old. She came to Japan (**al**   [2]), leaving all her (**fa**   [3]) members behind in her home country. Sato Yutaka and Harumi, living in Gunma, are helping her to adjust to life in Japan. Lena has been affected by the (**tr**   [4]) of war that she experienced in her country. The couple and other volunteers are working very hard to help her get used to living in Japan. Lena (**ap**   [5]) their efforts.

Listen to the News Story

CDの音声を聞いて、News Story の ❶～❼ の文中にある空所に適切な単語を書き入れましょう。音声は2回繰り返されます。

Anchor: More than 800 people have **fled** from Ukraine to Japan. Different levels of government are helping them with housing and living costs. But some evacuees don't have a personal connection to Japan and can't speak the language. In this next report, we will meet a family that's **stepping up** to help.

Narrator: Twenty-one-year-old Lena Berezhnaya moved to Gunma Prefecture near Tokyo last month, but she was alone in Japan. Her entire family is still in the Ukrainian city of Kharkiv, which has faced a **barrage** of attacks.

Lena Berezhnaya (Evacuee from Ukraine): I was scared because I didn't know when a missile would come flying, when I would be buried under the **debris**, and when and how I would lose my life.

Narrator: Berezhnaya decided to make the move after meeting a volunteer from Japan who was helping **refugees**. She was a fan of Japanese animation, so the country felt familiar.

Sato Yutaka and his wife Harumi became her host family.
❶ (¹) (²) (³)
(⁴) (⁵) (⁶),
so they use technology to communicate. They initially planned to host her until the authorities prepared a place for her to live, but they noticed she was struggling to **deal with** the **trauma** she'd experienced. So, they invited her to stay.

Sato Harumi (Berezhnaya's host): Lena has been very sensitive, even to the sound of [an] airplane or [a] helicopter.

Sato Yutaka (Berezhnaya's host): ❷ We couldn't just (¹)
(²), (³) (⁴)
(⁵) (⁶) (⁷).

Narrator: The family **makes sure** Berezhnaya is never alone. They've created a schedule so that someone is always around for her. They go shopping together so she can learn to navigate life in Japanese, even something as simple as buying vegetables.

❶ 彼らは共通の言語を話さない

❷ 彼女の幸運を願いながら、彼女のもとを去っていく

22

Sato Harumi: Mo-ya-shi (bean sprouts). Moyashi.

Berezhnaya: Moyashi?

Narrator: They also explain things that are different in Japan, like
paying with cash, which isn't as common in Ukraine. And
they are helping her stay active. On this day, they're visiting
a *zoo*.

Sato Harumi: Look at the camera, let's take a picture.

Narrator: ❸ Berezhnaya loves animals, so they are hoping it will

(¹) (²) (³)

(⁴) (⁵) (⁶)

at home.

❸ その状況を忘れる

Berezhnaya: I'm glad there are people like the Sato family.

❹ (¹) (²) (³)

(⁴) (⁵) (⁶).

❹ いつまでも彼らの
親切に感謝する

Sato Yutaka: **Cheers!**

❺ I think (¹) (²)

(³) (⁴) (⁵)

(⁶) (⁷).

❺ 彼女に実際必要な
ことは人々の支え
である

❻ We (¹) (²)

(³) (⁴) (⁵)

(⁶) (⁷) for Lena to live in

Japan.

❻ 快適な生活環境を
用意したい

Narrator: The Sato family plans to host Berezhnaya for as long as
she wants to stay. ❼ But they say their new friendship

(¹) (²) (³)

(⁴) (⁵) (⁶).

❼ 彼女の、次の動き
を超えて広がって
いく

Notes: (p. 22) ℓ. 24   airplane と helicopter の前に不定冠詞が必要
　　　(p. 23) ℓ. 6　（zoo について）協力・群馬サファリパーク
　　　　　　　ℓ. 7　この文は、ふつう2つの文で表す

各問、選択肢から適切な単語を選び、英文を完成させましょう。なお、余分な単語が1語ずつあります。

1. なつきは夜道で知らない人に後をつけられ怯えた。

Natsuki (＿＿＿＿＿＿) (＿＿＿＿＿＿) because a (＿＿＿＿＿) (＿＿＿＿＿) (＿＿＿＿＿) her on the (＿＿＿＿＿) at (＿＿＿＿＿).

| sidewalk | was | scared | following | frightening | stranger | night | was |

2. 先週の試合がどうなったか、クラブのメンバーみんなに必ず教えてね。

(＿＿＿＿＿) (＿＿＿＿＿) you (＿＿＿＿＿) every member of the club (＿＿＿＿＿) the (＿＿＿＿＿) (＿＿＿＿＿) (＿＿＿＿＿) week.

| competition | how | make | went | tell | believe | last | sure |

3. 仕事を終えてテレビで映画を見ると、職場でのストレスを忘れることができる。

Watching (＿＿＿＿＿) on TV (＿＿＿＿＿) my job helps (＿＿＿＿＿) my (＿＿＿＿＿) (＿＿＿＿＿) of stress at (＿＿＿＿＿).

| stress | mind | after | take | work | off | movies |

4. 面倒を見ると約束できるなら [～できる限りは]、新しい子犬をもらって来てあげてもいいよ。

I will (＿＿＿＿＿) (＿＿＿＿＿) a new puppy (＿＿＿＿＿) (＿＿＿＿＿) (＿＿＿＿＿) you (＿＿＿＿＿) to take (＿＿＿＿＿) of it.

| you | care | as | much | long | promise | as | get |

1. Where in Japan would you want to take foreign guests or travelers? Why? Explain.

2. If you were forced to suddenly move to another country, what would you miss most about your country? Name three things and explain.

UNIT 05 Mixing Art With Online Meetings

ズームアーティスト、松岡智子

MIXING ART WITH ONLINE MEETINGS

一般の会社員から芸術家へと転身した次世代アーティスト松岡智子氏がパリのアートフェア『サロン・アート・ショッピング・パリ』に初の海外出展を果たした。彼女の創作スタイルは、Zoom を利用してオンラインで会話をしながら、その人たちの価値観や資質などをペイントで抽象的に描く活動から始まった。

放送日 2022/6/9

Words & Phrases

CD 10

以下の単語や熟語の音声を聞きながら発音に注意し、意味を確認しましょう。

- □ pandemic　　　パンデミック、世界的感染病
- □ to remedy　　　〈欠点など〉を改善する、矯正する
- □ withdrawn　　　引きこもった、孤立した
  - 例文 After the death of his son, Bill became more and more *withdrawn*.
    息子が亡くなった後、ビルはますます引きこもってしまった。
- □ embodiment　　　具体的表現
- □ to commission　　　～を依頼する
- □ to turn A into B　　　A を B に変える
- □ to tap into　　　～を利用する
- □ intuition　　　直観力
- □ facial expression　　　表情
  - 例文 Our baby uses various *facial expressions* to show how she feels.
    私たちの赤ちゃんは感じ方によっていろいろな表情を示す[使う]。
- □ optimism　　　希望的観測、楽観主義
- □ scar-like　　　傷跡のような

以下は、芸術に関する表現です。下記の枠内から適切な単語を選び、空所に入れましょう。

- 美術 　　　　　　　　　　(　　　　　　　　 [1]) arts
- 抽象画 　　　　　　　　　(　　　　　　　　 [2]) art
- 静物画 　　　　　　　　　(　　　　　　　　 [3]) life
- 風景画 　　　　　　　　　(　　　　　　　　 [4]) painting
- 人物画 　　　　　　　　　(　　　　　　　　 [5])
- 宗教画 　　　　　　　　　(　　　　　　　　 [6]) painting
- 歴史画 　　　　　　　　　(　　　　　　　　 [7]) painting
- 浮世絵 　　　　　　　Japanese (　　　　　　　 [8]) print
- 風刺画 　　　　　　　　　(　　　　　　　　 [9])
- 油絵 　　　　　　　　　　(　　　　　　　　 [10]) painting
- 水彩画 　　　　　　　　　(　　　　　　　　 [11]) painting
- 漆器 　　　　　　　　　　(　　　　　　　　 [12]) ware
- 刺繍 　　　　　　　　　　(　　　　　　　　 [13])
- 彫刻 　　　　　　　　　　(　　　　　　　　 [14])
- 陶芸 　　　　　　　　　　(　　　　　　　　 [15])

abstract	caricature	embroidery	fine	historical
lacquer	landscape	oil	portrait	pottery
religious	sculpture	still	watercolor	woodblock

ニュースを見て、内容と合っているものは T 、違っているものは F を選びましょう。

1. Matsuoka tries to produce art that expresses the client's personality. 　　T・F

2. Kikegawa stopped working for a leisure facility company. 　　T・F

3. Matsuoka usually creates her art using a big mirror. 　　T・F

1 ニュースをもう一度見て、各問の空所に入る適切な選択肢を a ~ c から選びましょう。

1. Matsuoka _____.

   a. is an artist in her 30s

   b. used to work in a foreign country

   c. is teaching children how to draw pictures

2. Kikegawa _____.

   a. wanted to help people with low incomes

   b. hoped to help young people

   c. needed a new challenge

3. A scar-like image in Kikegawa's new background picture symbolizes his firm desire to _____.

   a. leave his past job

   b. make better money

   c. start his own company

2 右の文字列を並べ替えて単語を作り、各文の空所に入れて意味がとおるようにしましょう。一部の文字が与えてあるものもあります。

1. Matsuoka creates abstract artworks about people through (　　　　　　) interviews.　　　　　　　　　　　　　　　　　　　　　　[niloen]

2. Matsuoka enjoyed drawing (　　　　　　)《複数形》when she was a child.
　　　　　　　　　　　　　　　　　　　　　　　　　　　　　　　[itucreps]

3. In the interview with Kikegawa, Matsuoka wanted to know the main (　　　　　　) he quit his job.　　　　　　　　　　　　　　　[ansreo]

4. Making good artwork requires the combined efforts of artist and (　　　　　　).
　　　　　　　　　　　　　　　　　　　　　　　　　　　　　　　[tincle]

Listen to the News Story

CDの音声を聞いて、News Story の ❶〜❼ の文中にある空所に適切な単語を書き入れましょう。音声は2回繰り返されます。

Anchor: The coronavirus **pandemic** has forced many people to
lead more isolated lives. ❶ There's (¹)
(²) (³) (⁴)
(⁵) (⁶) (⁷).

5   Now a Japanese artist is aiming to remedy this through
creative online artworks.

Matsuoka Tomoko (Artist): (*To all the online participants*) Thank you for
today.

Narrator: This is Matsuoka Tomoko, a 33-year-old artist. She creates

10   background art displayed on computer monitors during
online meetings. She aims to make art that truly reflects the
individual's personality.

Matsuoka did not start out as an artist. After graduating, she
worked at a foreign-owned company but struggled to fit in.

15   She quit her job and became socially **withdrawn**. But then
she remembered the joy she felt as a child when she drew
pictures.

The turning point came in 2020 when a friend asked her to
draw a picture for her birthday. ❷ She (¹)

20   (²) (³) (⁴)
(⁵) (⁶) (⁷).

Matsuoka: I was wondering, "What am I living for?" But after I began
drawing, many people started saying, "It's okay."
❸ (¹) (²) (³)

25   (⁴) (⁵) (⁶)
(⁷), which is really what I most wanted to
hear.

Narrator: The concept behind Matsuoka's art is **embodiment** of the
spirit. She senses a range of emotions from the clients and

30   brings them to life through her visual creations.

This is Kikegawa Atsushi, age 54. ❹ He **commissioned** a

---

❶ 他の人たちと触れ合う機会が少ない

❷ アーティストになると決めた

❸ 自分は今のままで良い

❹ 印刷会社の仕事を辞めてから

background picture (¹) (²)
(³) (⁴) (⁵)
(⁶) of over 30 years to start a new role at a
leisure facility company.

5 *Kikegawa Atsushi (Client):* It's abstract art that captures a moment in time
using the artist's sensibility, but being able to **turn** it **into**
art gives it a very real sense of narrative. ❺ I think of it as
(¹) (²) (³)
(⁴) (⁵) (⁶)
10 (⁷).

Narrator: Matsuoka always creates her art in the presence of the client,
even if it's through a computer screen.

Matsuoka: What was the biggest reason for retiring from the company?
You wanted a new challenge?

15 *Kikegawa:* I wanted to help young people grow.

Narrator: While talking, she **taps into** her **intuition** to convey her
impressions on the canvas. It's a creative collaboration
between artist and client.

Matsuoka: I think this moment is very important for sensing various
20 things that go into my drawings, such as their **facial**
expressions or a change in their tone of voice, even when I'm
not directly looking at their face.

Narrator: This is Kikegawa's new background picture.
❻ (¹) (²) (³)
25 (⁴) (⁵) (⁶),
reflecting his hope and **optimism** in starting a new job. A
scar-like mark is a symbol of his determination to begin a
new chapter and leave his past behind.

Kikegawa: I think she described me in a new way, showing that I can
30 still do things and that I'm trying to break through a wall.

Matsuoka: I want to concretely express the client's many wonderful
qualities through art on the computer screen.

Narrator: ❼ It's a timely and (¹) (²)
(³) (⁴) (⁵)
35 (⁶), offering a new way for people to connect
in pandemic times.

❺ 自分の歴史を記録
する一つの方法

❻ それは明るい〜色
に塗られている

❼ 現代の世界にとっ
て独創的な方法の
到来である

各問、選択肢から適切な単語を選び、英文を完成させましょう。なお、余分な単語が1語ずつあります。

1. 美咲は懸命に努力して、できる限り最高の顧客サービス係になることを<u>目指している</u>。

   Misaki works hard and (＿＿＿＿＿＿＿＿) (＿＿＿＿＿＿＿＿) be the best (＿＿＿＿＿＿＿＿)
   service (＿＿＿＿＿＿) she (＿＿＿＿＿＿) (＿＿＿＿＿＿).

can	to	customer	be	aims	on	representative

2. 真紀は新しいクラスメートたちとうまくいっているようだ。同年代のみんなの中によく<u>溶け込</u><u>ん</u>でいると思う。

   Maki seems to be (＿＿＿＿) (＿＿＿＿＿) well (＿＿＿＿＿) her new
   classmates. I think she (＿＿＿＿＿＿) right (＿＿＿＿＿＿) with people her
   (＿＿＿＿＿).

fits	getting	with	old	in	age	along

3. 誠は、ユニクロや無印良品<u>など</u>で<u>売られている</u>あまり高くない洋服（を着るの）が好きだ。

   Makoto (＿＿＿＿＿) to (＿＿＿＿＿) (＿＿＿＿＿)-priced clothes (＿＿＿＿＿＿)
   (＿＿＿＿＿＿) those (＿＿＿＿＿) (＿＿＿＿＿) Uniqlo and MUJI.

by	loves	as	so	reasonably	such	sold	wear

4. 自分の<u>過去</u>を<u>捨て</u>たいのなら、そのためのベストの方法は、以前犯したあやまちを繰り返さない [避ける] ことである。

   If you want to (＿＿ ＿＿＿) your (＿＿＿＿＿＿) (＿＿＿＿＿＿), the
   best (＿＿＿＿＿) to do it is to (＿＿＿＿＿) the (＿＿＿＿＿) you
   (＿＿＿＿＿) before.

behind	repeat	mistakes	made	leave	way	past	avoid

1. What kinds of jobs are you interested in? Why?

2. What kind of art do you like better: fine arts, like painting, or performing arts, like music? Why?

30

UNIT 06

Deer Ramen

山梨ジビエラーメン

NHK WORLD JAPAN
LINE ASIA 24

DEER RAMEN GIVES VILLAGE NEW HOPE

人口530人程の山梨県丹波山村（たばやまむら）では、ジビエを使った料理が開発されている。最も成功しているのが鹿骨からだしをとった「鹿ラーメン」で、味に特徴を出すため試行錯誤の末、事業を黒字に転換した。それまで廃棄していた部位を余すところなく利用するために他の商品も手掛け、おかげで村の認知度も上昇している。

放送日 2022/6/29

Words & Phrases

○ CD 12

以下の単語や熟語の音声を聞きながら発音に注意し、意味を確認しましょう。

☐ **lush** 〈植物が〉青々と茂った
☐ to **forage** 〈食糧などを〉探し回る
☐ to **head up** 〜を指揮する
例文 He is *heading up* the task force.
　　彼は対策本部を率いている。
☐ **broth** だし汁
☐ **venison** 鹿肉
☐ **bark** 樹皮
☐ to **devour** 〜を貪り食う
☐ **meat scrap** 肉の切れ端
☐ **gamy** （猟鳥獣の肉が）やや匂う
☐ **savory** 風味のある、味の良い
☐ **cuisine** 料理
例文 We spent the evening sampling the local *cuisine*.
　　私たちは地元の料理を味わいながら夕方を過ごした。

Before You Watch

以下は、ラーメンに関する表現や説明です。下の枠内から適切な単語を選び、空所に入れましょう。なお、余分な単語もあります。

1. 醬油ラーメン　　　　　　　　（　　　　　　　　　） ramen

2. 塩ラーメン　　　　　　　　　（　　　　　　　　　） ramen

3. 味噌ラーメン　　　　　　　　（　　　　　　　　　） ramen

4. 豚骨ラーメン　　　　　　　　ramen in (　　　　　　　　) soup

5. つけ麺　　　　　　　　　　　noodles with a (　　　　　　　) sauce

6. チャーシュー　　　　　　　　（　　　　　　　　） pork

7. メンマ　　　　　　　　　　　（　　　　　　　　） shoot

8. ねぎ　　　　　　　　　　　　（　　　　　　　　） onion

9. もやし　　　　　　　　　　　（　　　　　　　　） sprout

10. 海苔　　　　　　　　　　　　（　　　　　　　　） seaweed

11. 大盛り　　　　　　　　　　　large (　　　　　　　　)

12. 替え玉　　　　　　　　　　　extra (　　　　　　　　) of noodles

13. このラーメンのおつゆはあっさりしている。　　This ramen soup is (　　　　　　　).

14. このラーメンのおつゆはコクがある。　This ramen soup has a (　　　　　　　) taste.

15. このラーメンの麺は細くて縮れている。　These ramen noodles are thin and (　　　　　).

16. 麺は柔らかめでお願いします。　　I'd like (　　　　　　　) noodles, please.

17. 日本では麺をすするときに音を立てるのはかまわない。

　　　　　　　　　　　　In Japan, it's okay to (　　　　　　　) your noodles.

> bamboo　　bean　　dipping　　firm　　green　　grilled　　heavy　　helping
> laver　　light　　pork-bone-based　　rich　　salt-flavored　　serving
> slurp　　soft　　soybean-flavored　　soy-sauce-flavored　　thick　　wavy

1st Viewing ≫ Watch the News

ニュースを見て、内容と合っているものは T 、違っているものは F を選びましょう。

1. Deer often damage trees and farmers' crops.　　　　　　　　　　T・F

2. Until recently, people used less than a quarter of a deer's meat.　　T・F

3. Hosaka used a food truck to sell his deer ramen.　　　　　　　　T・F

2nd Viewing >> Understand the News

1 ニュースをもう一度見て、各問の空所に入る適切な選択肢を a～c から選びましょう。

1. Hosaka utilized meat scraps for _____.

   a. hamburgers
   b. curry
   c. spaghetti sauce

2. To make the broth richer, Hosaka _____.

   a. tried different gas flame levels
   b. mixed in chicken stock
   c. added a lot of olive oil

Hosaka Yukinori
CEO, At home supporters

3. In the future, Hosaka wants to start a school which specializes in _____.

   a. producing mounted animals
   b. hunting large animals
   c. processing wild animals

2 以下はニュースの概要です。空所に適切な単語を書き入れましょう。語頭の文字（群）は与えてあります。

In Tabayama Village, Yamanashi Prefecture, dishes using deer meat have recently been developed. Hosaka, CEO at a (**l** [1]) food processing company, came up with the idea of producing food items, such as (**cr** [2]). His most successful dish is deer ramen, which is made from deer (**b** [3]) broth and roasted deer meat. Improving the broth was a matter of (**t** [4]) and error, and he finally succeeded in producing a (**dis** [5]), savory ramen. Hosaka made full use of the parts of deer that had usually been discarded and hopes to make his village famous for deer ramen.

Listen to the News Story

CDの音声を聞いて、News Story の ❶〜❼ の文中にある空所に適切な単語を書き入れましょう。音声は2回繰り返されます。

Anchor: Deer are so familiar to the Japanese that they even appear in traditional poetry. ❶ However, recently, they are seen as harmful animals that (¹) (²) (³) (⁴) (⁵) (⁶) (⁷).
5   We focus on the efforts of one small village that's reversing the harmful effects of these wild animals, and in the process, making something quite tasty.

❶ 森や穀物に損害を及ぼす

Narrator: Deep in the **lush** green mountains of Yamanashi, it's no
10   wonder that deer **forage** for food around Tabayama Village. Hosaka Yukinori **heads up** a local food processing company. He recently hit upon a new dish, featuring deer. It's called deer ramen and is made with deer bone **broth** and roasted deer meat or **venison**.

15   **Hosaka Yukinori** *(CEO, At home supporters):* I thought that we could get our village on the map if we served deer ramen. ❷ My biggest desire is (¹) (²) (³) (⁴) (⁵) (⁶) Tabayama.

❷ 〜という名前を人々に認知される

20   *Narrator:*   Deer are often targeted for hunting because they peel tree **bark** and **devour** crops. ❸ Until recently, (¹) (²) (³) (⁴) (⁵) (⁶) (⁷) and used just 25 percent of each animal. ❹ Such waste made it (¹)
25   (²) (³) (⁴) (⁵) (⁶).

❸ 地元住民が肉だけのためにそれらを狩猟した

❹ 利益の上がる商売とは程遠い

At first, Hosaka used **meat scraps** to develop croquettes, curry and even pet food. He then turned his attention to deer
30   bones to make broth. But Hosaka faced a big problem. His

34

soup wasn't **gamy**, but it lacked a rich, **savory** flavor.

Hosaka: My biggest challenge was that I couldn't detect any distinct flavor.

Narrator: To increase the broth's richness, Hosaka added more bones to his soup. He also tried various gas flame levels and boiling times. After a year of trial and error, he finally found the perfect combination. The utilization rate per deer soared to 75 percent, and the market price of deer went up as well. And that's given village authorities high hopes for deer products in the future.

Isobe Tomohiro (Tabayama Village Official): ❺ ([1])
([2]) ([3]) ([4])
([5]) ([6]) ([7])
where Tabayama is located. ❻ My hope is that
([1]) ([2]) ([3])
([4]) ([5]) ([6])
([7]) for deer **cuisine**.

Narrator: Hosaka launched a promotion of his deer ramen using a food truck.

Hosaka: Meat is only one part of the deer. ❼ We ([1])
([2]) ([3]) ([4])
([5]) ([6]) ([7])
to eliminate any waste. I hope our way will become popular nationwide.

Narrator: To achieve that goal, Hosaka wants to open a school specializing in animal processing.

❺ 今までほとんどの
人たちに良い考え
が浮かばなかった

❻ 私たちの村が旅行
者の目的地になる

❼ 鹿一頭まるまる使
い切ろうとする

Review the Key Expressions

各問、選択肢から適切な単語を選び、英文を完成させましょう。なお、余分な単語が１語ずつあります。

1. 自分の車が盗難され（てい）たのを知り、彼はあまりにびっくりして口がきけなかった。

   When he (　　　　　) that his car (　　　　　) (　　　　　)
   (　　　　　), he was (＿＿＿＿＿) upset (＿＿＿＿＿) he (　　　　　)
   not speak.

had	so	discovered	been	that	could	someone	stolen

2. 彼は自分の生まれ故郷についての本を出版しようと思いついた。

   He (＿＿＿＿＿) (＿＿＿＿＿) the (　　　　　) of (　　　　　) a
   (　　　　　) about his (　　　　　).

hometown	book	called	hit	publishing	idea	upon

3. 孤独は彼が外国で直面した最も大変な問題だった。

   (　　　　　) was the (　　　　　) (　　　　　) problem (　　　　　)
   (＿＿＿＿＿) in (　　　　　) countries.

most	loneliness	faced	foreign	asked	severe	he

4. 私は試行錯誤して、自分の新しいスマホの使い方を学んだ。

   I learned (　　　　　) (　　　　　) (　　　　　) my new (　　　　　)
   (　　　　　) (＿＿＿＿＿) and (＿＿＿＿＿).

by	change	how	error	smartphone	operate	trial	to

Discussion Questions

1. Do you like either regular ramen or instant ramen? If so, what flavor do you like the best? If not, why not?

2. If you could start your own business, what kind of company would you choose? Why?

UNIT 07

Making Sure the Message Is Heard

英語で語り継ぐ

GUIDES EXPLAIN A-BOMB DEVASTATION IN ENGLISH

広島の多くの人がボランティアで外国人観光客のガイドをしている。被爆者の話を広めることでロシアのウクライナ侵攻と核兵器の脅威が進む今、全世界の人への警告として役立つと考えている。核兵器の恐ろしさを伝えられるのは、生存者と彼らから直接学んだ人だけである。彼らは自分の視点を追加して次世代に伝える責任があると考えている。

放送日 2022/8/3

Words & Phrases

CD 14

以下の単語や熟語の音声を聞きながら発音に注意し、意味を確認しましょう。

☐ **worthwhile**　　価値のある

例文 "Ron's Gone Wrong" is a *worthwhile* film for both children and adults.
「ロン 僕のポンコツ・ロボット」は子供にも大人にも見る価値のある映画だ。

☐ to **be involved**　　〈活動などに〉参加する、関わる

☐ **in particular**　　特に

☐ **devastation**　　破壊

☐ to **take**〈something〉**for granted**　　〜を当然と考える

☐ **perspective**　　見方、見解

☐ to **cut down on**　　〜を減らす

例文 He is trying to *cut down on* smoking.
彼は喫煙量を減らそうとしている。

☐ **all the more**　　（それだけ）なおさら

☐ **recollection**　　回想

☐ to **deter**　　阻止する

☐ to **remind**〈someone〉**of**　　〈人に〉〜を思い出させる

Before You Watch

英語はstress accent（強弱アクセント）を使う言語です。下記は本単元に出てくる単語ですが、第1アクセントの位置や、発音に関して間違いやすいものをリストしてあります。A〜Kの各単語について適切な発音を選び、空所に番号を入れましょう。

A. **atomic**　　1. átomic　　2. atómic　　3. atomíc　　　　（　　　　）

B. **urgent**　　1. úrgent　　2. urgént　　　　　　　　　　（　　　　）

C. **prevent**　　1. prévent　　2. prevént　　　　　　　　（　　　　）

D. **particular**　1. párticular　2. partícular　3. particulár　（　　　　）

E. **devastation**　1. dévastation　2. devástation　3. devastátion　（　　　　）

F. **deter**　　1. déter　　2. detér　　　　　　　　　　　（　　　　）

G. **nuclear**　　1. núclear　　2. nucléar　　3. nucleár　（　　　　）

H. **remind**　　1. rémind　　2. remínd　　　　　　　　（　　　　）

I. **impact**《名詞》　1. ímpact　　2. impáct　　　　　　（　　　　）

J. **message**　　1. message [mésɪdʒ]　　2. message [mesé:dʒ]　（　　　　）

K. **bombing**　　1. bombing [bάmɪŋ]　　2. bombing [bάmbɪŋ]　（　　　　）

1st Viewing ≫ Watch the News

ニュースを見て、内容と合っているものはT、違っているものはFを選びましょう。

1. Some 30 students volunteered as guides for travelers from abroad.　　　 T・F

2. International students don't know much about the atomic bomb dropped on Hiroshima.　　　 T・F

3. As an elementary school student, Ogura Keiko survived the atomic bombing of Hiroshima.　　　 T・F

2nd Viewing >> Understand the News

1 ニュースをもう一度見て、各問の空所に入る適切な選択肢を a ~ c から選びましょう。

1. Yagi Mayuko is a college student majoring in _____.

   a. business administration
   b. literature
   c. tourism

2. Ogura Keiko says that to _____ is important for effective communication.

   a. learn visitors' backgrounds
   b. use a translation device
   c. speak to small groups

3. Yagi Mayuko thinks it is necessary to _____.

   a. read the tour manual aloud to tourists
   b. have heart-to-heart communication with visitors
   c. record the questions that tourists ask during tours

2 以下はニュースの概要です。空所に適切な単語を書き入れましょう。語頭の文字（群）は与えてあります。

Many people in Hiroshima are volunteering to guide tourists from (**ov**   [1]). The volunteers believe that spreading the stories of the atomic bomb (**sur**   [2])《複数形》, like Ogura Keiko, will serve as a warning to people all over the world, as Russia's invasion of (**U**   [3]) and the threat of nuclear war are happening now. The horrors of nuclear weapons can only be conveyed by people who have survived or those who have seriously studied about them. As a (**c**   [4]) student guide, Yagi Mayuko wants to directly talk with her international audience in the (**E**   [5]) language.

CDの音声を聞いて、News Story の ❶〜❼ の文中にある空所に適切な単語を書き入れましょう。音声は2回繰り返されます。

Anchor: Learning another language is always **worthwhile**. For students in Hiroshima though, it's an urgent matter. They're working to convey the history of what happened there in 1945 to prevent it from happening again anywhere in the world. Here's a report on their efforts.

5

Yagi Mayuko (Guide): ❶ The (¹) (²) (³) (⁴) (⁵) (⁶) from the bridge …

❶ 原爆が〜メートル離れたところで爆発する

Narrator: Students **make** good **use of** their best English in guiding tourists from overseas. About 50 of them have been volunteering for this project. They come from both high school and college. Yagi Mayuko has been **involved** for three years. She's studying tourism at a university. She felt that international students **in particular** needed a better understanding of the atomic bomb **devastation**.

10

15

Yagi: I realized that exchange students knew very little about the atomic bombing, information that I **took for granted**, so I decided to become a tour guide and offer them my **perspective** as a Hiroshima native.

Narrator: Between classes, she studies English and prepares for a tour.

20

Yagi: I'm double-checking how a native speaker would pronounce "atomic bomb." ❷ (¹) (²) (³) (⁴) (⁵) (⁶). If my pronunciation is wrong, people won't understand me.

❷ 常にアクセントやイントネーションを学習している

25

Narrator: The COVID pandemic **cut down on** the number of tours, but the team expects more visitors this year, and the possible use of nuclear weapons in Ukraine makes the lessons of Hiroshima **all the more** important.

Recently, the members listened to the **recollections** of Ogura Keiko, an atomic bomb survivor.

30

Ogura Keiko: I was eight years old when the bomb was dropped. ❸ I *wear* the burning clothes and the burned skin (¹) (²) (³) (⁴) (⁵) (⁶) (⁷).

5   Don't you see? *At* that direction …

Narrator: Ogura emphasized understanding the background of visitors in order to communicate with them effectively.

Yagi: The world is facing another war. My perspective is one that only atomic bomb survivors or those who have

10   studied the bomb's devastation can provide. ❹ I want to (¹) (²) (³) (⁴) (⁵) (⁶) and **deter** the use of nuclear weapons.

Narrator: Yagi thought hard about a question she was asked during a

15   tour for trainees of an international organization.

Student: *Tell me about it, a history, a painful history of your country.* How are you feeling? A painful part of the history of Japan.

Yagi: Every time I heard the painful story, I think that I should do something …

20 *Narrator:* The question **reminded** her **of** the need to communicate heart-to-heart.

Yagi: ❺ I want to speak directly to my audience in English, without looking at the script (¹) (²) (³) (⁴) (⁵)

25   (⁶) (⁷). ❻ And I hope the international visitors in turn (¹) (²) (³) (⁴) (⁵) (⁶) who know nothing about the atomic bomb.

30 *Narrator:* ❼ The message is being delivered by her and others much younger (¹) (²) (³) (⁴) (⁵) (⁶) (⁷).

---

❸ 最初の爆弾でやられた

❹ できるだけ多くの人に接触して

❺ 言いたいことがもっとインパクトがあるように

❻ お話をほかの人たちに伝える

❼ 多くの聞き手が理解できる言語で

Notes: (p. 41) ℓ. 2　wore が文法的に正しい　ℓ. 5　In がしぜん
　　　　ℓ. 16　あまり明瞭ではないので、著者が補った箇所

Review the Key Expressions

各問、選択肢から適切な単語を選び、英文を完成させましょう。なお、余分な単語が1語ずつあります。

1. 昼のあいだ眠くなるので、私は夜働く時間を削減しようしている。

   I'm (　　　　　) to (＿＿＿＿＿) (　　　　　) (＿＿＿＿＿) the number
   of hours I work at (　　　　　) because I (　　　　　) (　　　　　)
   during the day.

   | sleepy | cut | on | at | night | feel | trying | down |

2. 先進国のほとんどの人たちは、1日3食食べられることを当然だと思っている。

   Most people in (　　　　　) (　　　　　) (＿＿＿＿＿) it (　　　　　)
   (＿＿＿＿＿) that (　　　　　) can eat three meals a (　　　　　).

   | developing | granted | advanced | for | day | they | countries | take |

3. これらの写真はいつも5年前（過ごした）アメリカの夏休みを思い出させる。

   These (　　　　　) always (＿＿＿＿＿) (　　　　　) (＿＿＿＿＿) my
   (　　　　　) (　　　　　) in America five years (　　　　　).

   | summer | ago | me | pictures | vacation | remind | remember | of |

4. 忠犬ハチはご主人の死を何も知らずに、来る日も来る日も渋谷駅で待っていた。

   The (　　　　　) dog Hachi (＿＿＿＿＿) (　　　　　) (　　　　　)
   his master's (　　　　　) and (　　　　　) for his owner day after
   (　　　　　) at Shibuya Station.

   | knew | faithful | death | nothing | night | day | waited | about |

Discussion Questions

1. What is the most memorable tour you have taken? When and where did you go? Explain.

2. In your opinion, is learning English important for you or Japanese people? Why or why not?

UNIT 08

Think Globally, Graze Locally

飼料高騰にライ麦

NFLATION SPURS INNOVATION IN FEED SOURCE

牛などの家畜の飼料輸入価格が高騰している。中国国内での需要の増加や南米での不作に加えて、穀類の主要産地であるウクライナの戦争がこの状況を悪化させると懸念されている。その対策として酪農で有名な北海道、音更町（おとふけちょう）では、これまでほとんど栽培されていないライ麦に活路を見いだそうと注目が集まっている。

放送日 2022/7/4

Words & Phrases

 CD 16

以下の単語や熟語の音声を聞きながら発音に注意し、意味を確認しましょう。

- ☐ to **graze**　　〈家畜が〉草を食べる
- ☐ **feed**　　飼料
- ☐ **dairy farmer**　　酪農家
- ☐ **alternative**　　代わりになるもの、代用品
- ☐ to **come up with**　　〜を思いつく
   例文 The young inventor *came up with* an ingenious idea.
   若い発明家は独創的な考えを思いついた。
- ☐ **Ukraine** [jukréɪn]　　ウクライナ
- ☐ **circumstance**　　状況
- ☐ to **fix**　　〜を固定させる
- ☐ to **stand up to**　　〜に強い、に立ち向かう
- ☐ **under control**　　収まって、制御されて
   例文 The pandemic is not yet *under control*.
   その世界的流行病はまだ収まっていない。

Before You Watch

以下は、語源に関する問題です。下の選択肢から日本語を選び表の空所に入れましょう。

	語彙	意味	形態素	意味	形態素	意味	形態素	意味
（例）	**introduce**	紹介する	**intro–**	中に	**–duce**	導く		
1	percent	パーセント	per–		–cent			
2	international	国際的な	inter–		–nation–		–al	〜の
3	circumstance	状況	circum–		–stance			
4	agriculture	農業	agri–		–culture			
5	imported		im–		–port–	運ぶ	–ed	〜された
6	domestic		domest–	家族	–ic			
7	prefer	〜の方を好む	pre–		–fer			
8	avoidable	避けられる	a–	〜を離れて	–void–		–able	
9	solution	解決法	solu–		–tion			
10	associate		as–	〜のほうへ	–soci–		–ate	〜する

> 国家　　前に　　国産の　　〜につき　　〜の
> 　〜の間の　　交際する　　空にする　　こと　　社会
> 　　まわりに　　〜できる　　100　　栽培　　中に
> 　立っていること　　〜を輸入された　　〜を溶かす　　運ぶ　　畑

1st Viewing >> ## Watch the News

ニュースを見て、内容と合っているものはT、違っているものはFを選びましょう。

1. Dairy farmer Yamada Akiyoshi has more than 500 cows.　　　T・F

2. According to farmer Ishikawa, it is not easy to produce rye.　　　T・F

3. Researcher Kon tested whether cows prefer rye to grass.　　　T・F

1 ニュースをもう一度見て、各問の空所に入る適切な選択肢を a～c から選びましょう。

1. The price Yamada paid for cattle feed in 2021 was
   _____.

   a. about the same as two years before
   b. around 30 percent higher than in 2020
   c. half as much as in 2018

2. _____ available to help dairy farmers.

   a. Large, low-interest loans were
   b. A local group of volunteers was
   c. Financial support from the local government was

Yamada Akiyoshi
Dairy farmer

3. Yamada thinks dairy farmers want to _____.

   a. use locally-grown feed for their cattle
   b. reduce the number of cows they own
   c. find countries that sell cheaper feed

2 以下はニュースの概要です。空所に適切な単語を書き入れましょう。語頭の文字（群）は与えてあります。

The price of cattle (**fe**   [1]) has been rising recently. In Japan, most farmers rely on imports for grass. (**Da**   [2]) farmers are having a hard time surviving. The small town of Otofuke in Hokkaido has been looking for a solution. They didn't used to grow (**r**   [3]) locally, but they started looking into the product as a possible (**al**   [4]) to grass. The plant is easy to grow, even in the (**c**   [5]) weather. Cows also seem to (**pre**   [6]) the taste of the plant to that of grass. If the project succeeds, the cows, farmers and consumers will all be happy.

Listen to the News Story

CDの音声を聞いて、News Story の ❶〜❼ の文中にある空所に適切な単語を書き入れましょう。音声は2回繰り返されます。

Anchor: Rising **feed** prices have Japanese **dairy farmers** searching for **alternatives** to imported products. A town in Hokkaido thinks it has, it is, it has **come up with** a solution, a different plant that can be grown right there. NHK World's Yonezawa Naoki reports.

Narrator: Imported grass feed is on *the* menu for many of Yamada Akiyoshi's 620 cows.

Yamada Akiyoshi (Dairy farmer): I've been worried since last year.

❶ (¹) (²) (³)
(⁴) (⁵) (⁶)
(⁷).

Narrator: Yamada's feed costs in 2021 were about 30 percent higher than the year before. The situation in **Ukraine** may make matters worse.

Yamada: The increasing cost of imported feed is tied up with unavoidable international **circumstances**. The prices of dairy products are **fixed** though. ❷ I'm not sure
(¹) (²) (³)
(⁴) (⁵) (⁶).

Narrator: The town of Otofuke is looking for an alternative.

❸ (¹) (²) (³)
(⁴) (⁵) (⁶)
for the first time. ❹ Otofuke and its agricultural
association started (¹) (²)
(³) (⁴) (⁵)
(⁶) (⁷).

Rye **stands up to** cold weather, so it can be grown in fields that have not been used in winter. Those who raise it then can sell it to dairy farmers.

❶ 草の価格が高騰し続けている

❷ 農家を継続できるか

❸ ライ麦は、〜月に収穫された

❹ 〜年ほど前にライ麦を調査することを…

46

Ishikawa Takashi (Farmer): Rye is easy to harvest, and it will support dairy

    farmers. ❺ I (¹) (²)

    (³) (⁴) (⁵)

    (⁶) (⁷).

₅ *Narrator:* The cows should be happy too.

Kon Akihito (Hokkaido Animal Research Center): We fed both grass and rye to the

    cows over a day. They didn't eat much of the grass and

    obviously preferred rye. ❻ I think the harvesting of rye

    domestically will be (¹) (²)

₁₀   (³) (⁴) (⁵)

    (⁶) (⁷).

Narrator: Financial support from the town and the association is

    keeping costs **under control**.

Yamada: ❼ I think rye is (¹) (²)

₁₅   (³) (⁴) (⁵)

    (⁶) (⁷). We want to use

    what can be harvested locally.

Narrator: If the project is successful, the cows, the *farms* and consumers

    will all be content. Yonezawa Naoki, NHK World.

---

❺ この仕事を推し進
   める計画である

❻ 酪農家にとって大
   きな前進 (となる)

❼ 家畜のえさのため
   の妥当な選択肢

Notes: (p. 46) ℓ. 6　正しくはこのようにthe になる
      (p. 47) ℓ. 18　*farms* は farmers とすべき

Review the Key Expressions

各問、選択肢から適切な単語を選び、英文を完成させましょう。なお、余分な単語が1語ずつあります。

1. 最高経営責任者は、社員たちの賃金を5年で倍増させる驚くべき計画案を思いついた。

   The CEO has (　　　　　) (　　　　　) (　　　　　) an amazing
   (　　　　　) to (　　　　　) his employees' (　　　　　) (　　　　　)
   five years.

double	come	in	wages	with	triple	scheme	up

2. 私たちは道に迷い、山のふもとに戻れなくなったが、さらに悪いことに、雨まで降り出してきた。

   We (　　　　　) our (　　　　　) (　　　　　) to the (　　　　　) of
   the mountain, and, to (　　　　　) (　　　　　) (　　　　　), it began to
   rain.

foot	top	matters	lost	way	worse	back	make

3. ウクライナの大統領は、戦争の状況を話し合うために初めて広島を訪れた。

   The president of Ukraine (　　　　　) Hiroshima (　　　　　) (　　　　　)
   (　　　　　) (　　　　　) to (　　　　　) about the war (　　　　　).

with	talk	for	time	visited	the	situation	first

4. 首相は、何も達成していないと言っている評論家たちに対して否定して [立ち向かって] いる。

   The Prime Minister (　　　　　) (　　　　　) to (　　　　　) who
   (　　　　　) he (　　　　　) (　　　　　) anything.

accomplished	say	up	critics	hasn't	looks	stands

Discussion Questions

1. Are you interested in farming? If yes, which would you prefer to do: grow vegetables or raise farm animals? Why? If you aren't interested in farming, why not?

2. Many people feel that living expenses are too high. What do you do to save money? Explain. If you don't do anything, why not?

A Sea Turtle's Tale

ウミガメの絵本

SEA TURTLE'S TALE

ウミガメが海洋ごみで右前足を失った。見つかった時にはこのカメはほぼ瀕死の状態だった。みんなの努力のおかげで、リハビリを経てなんとか海に戻ることができたが、海洋汚染の深刻さがあらわになった。今回のウミガメの問題で絵本の発行を思いつき、住民の意識と行動に進展が見られた。

放送日 2022/9/20

Words & Phrases

CD 18

以下の単語や熟語の音声を聞きながら発音に注意し、意味を確認しましょう。

☐ **debris**　　　　がれき
☐ to **persist**　　　存続する、存在する
例文 Her cough *persisted* for two weeks.
　　 彼女の咳は2週間も続いた。
☐ **tangled**　　　　絡まった、もつれた
☐ **ordeal**　　　　苦しい体験
☐ **limb**　　　　　手足（の1本）
☐ to **constrict**　　〜を締め付ける、抑制する
☐ **distress**　　　　（肉体的）苦しみ、苦痛
☐ **droppings**　　　（鳥獣類の）ふん、排泄物
☐ **plight**　　　　苦境、窮地
☐ to **cherish**　　　〜を大切にする
例文 This is a country where people *cherish* their traditions.
　　 ここは自分たちの伝統を重んじる国である。
☐ **jellyfish**　　　くらげ

以下は、環境問題に関する語彙です。下の枠内から適切な単語を選び、空所に入れましょう。

1. 海洋汚染　　　　　　　　　sea (　　　　　　　　　)

2. 環境に優しい　　　　　　　environmentally-(　　　　　　　　　)

3. 気候変動　　　　　　　　　(　　　　　　　　　) change

4. 環境活動家　　　　　　　　environmental (　　　　　　　　　)

5. 環境への負荷　　　　　　　environmental (　　　　　　　　　)

6. 天然資源　　　　　　　　　(　　　　　　　　　) resources

7. 温室効果ガス　　　　　　　(　　　　　　　　　) gas

8. 再生可能エネルギー　　　　(　　　　　　　　　) energy

9. マイバッグ[再利用できるバッグ]　(　　　　　　　　　) bags

10. 持続可能な生活スタイル　　(　　　　　　　　　) lifestyle

11. 地球温暖化　　　　　　　　global (　　　　　　　　　)

12. 有害廃棄物　　　　　　　　(　　　　　　　　　) waste

13. 森林破壊　　　　　　　　　(　　　　　　　　　)

14. 化石燃料　　　　　　　　　(　　　　　　　　　) fuel

15. 原子力発電　　　　　　　　(　　　　　　　　　) power generation

activist	climate	deforestation	footprint	fossil
friendly	greenhouse	hazardous	natural	nuclear
pollution	renewable	reusable	sustainable	warming

ニュースを見て、内容と合っているものはＴ、違っているものはＦを選びましょう。

1. The picture book about Liv is based on a real story.　　　　T・F

2. People in Okinawa were cleaning up their local beaches.　　T・F

3. Saving the sea for future generations is one of the messages of this picture book.

T・F

2nd Viewing >> **Understand the News**

1 ニュースをもう一度見て、各問の空所に入る適切な選択肢を a ~ c から選びましょう。

1. People cleaned up beaches and collected one hundred _____ that year.

   a. kinds of fishing nets
   b. kilograms of plastic bags
   c. tons of debris

2. The nursery school kids _____.

   a. put on a play about Liv
   b. learned how to make fishing nets
   c. thought of ways to make turtles happy

Abe Yuki
Okinokuni Diving

3. One of the problems about sea turtles is that they _____.

   a. tend to overeat
   b. consume too many jellyfish
   c. eat plastic products by mistake

2 ニュースをもう一度見て、以下の各情報を、物事が起こった順番に並べましょう。

1. The team, including Abe Yuki, took care of Liv.

2. A picture book about the sea turtle was published.

3. The sea turtle recovered and was returned to the sea.

4. An injured sea turtle was found in a net.

CDの音声を聞いて、News Story の ❶〜❼ の文中にある空所に適切な単語を書き入れましょう。音声は2回繰り返されます。

Anchor: In our next report, we meet Liv, the sea turtle.

❶ (¹) (²) (³)
(⁴) (⁵) (⁶)
in Japan after being severely injured by sea **debris**. Now a
picture book of her true story is touching the hearts of many,
highlighting the reality of marine pollution and inspiring
them to step up. Here's a closer look.

❶ 彼女［ウミガメ］は海岸で救助された

Narrator: This story takes place on Okinoshima Island. I'm a sea turtle,
named Liv by the humans who hoped I would survive after
rescuing me.

This story is set on an island off the coast of Shimane
Prefecture. ❷ It's based on the true story of Liv, the
sea turtle rescued two years ago (¹)
(²) (³) (⁴)
(⁵) (⁶). Abe Yuki is one of
the *team* who took care of Liv, leading to the creation of this
picture book.

❷ 最後には海に戻された

Abe Yuki (Okinokuni Diving): Liv recovered, but the waste problem **persists**.

❸ (¹) (²) (³)
(⁴) (⁵) (⁶)
through the book.

❸ 私はこの問題に対処したいと思った

Narrator: Liv was washed ashore on the island after becoming **tangled**
in a fishing net.

"I lost my hand."

Weakened by the **ordeal**, she lost one of her **limbs** after
being tightly **constricted** by the net.

Here is Liv at that time. ❹ Abe describes (¹)
(²) (³) (⁴)
(⁵) (⁶) (⁷)
due to her injuries. Liv was also in **distress** due to pieces of
plastic that were found in her **droppings**. The turtle's **plight**

❹ 彼女がどのように苦しんでいるようだったか

raised environmental awareness among locals.

After watching Liv suffer, they're inspired to clean up their beaches. They collected about one hundred tons of debris in a year.

⁵ Younger residents also felt an increased respect for the ocean. Children at this nursery school performed a play based on Liv's story. ❺ They also (¹)
(²) (³) (⁴)
(⁵) (⁶).

❺ 海岸のごみを掃除した

¹⁰ ❻ Today (¹) (²)
(³) (⁴) (⁵)
(⁶) (⁷) to the children.

❻ この絵本が朗読された

Nursery Teacher: I hope they will continue to **cherish** and preserve our beautiful ocean.

¹⁵ *Narrator:* The book ends with a scene in which Liv, having recovered, returns to the sea. ❼ (¹) (²)
(³) (⁴) (⁵)
(⁶) (⁷) (⁸).

❼ しかし、これは典型的なハッピーな終わり方ではない

The **jellyfish** and a plastic bag can clearly be seen next to
²⁰ Liv, highlighting how the issue of sea waste is not resolved.

Abe: Many turtles eat plastic bags, thinking that they're jellyfish. But there are now more people who are willing to clean up than before, and I think Liv would be happy about that.

Narrator: Liv not only showed strength and courage in recovering. The
²⁵ incident also taught humans a valuable lesson about marine debris and the importance of preserving the sea for future generations.

Note: （p. 52）ℓ. 16　*team* は team members とするのが正しい

各問、選択肢から適切な単語を選び、英文を完成させましょう。なお、余分な単語が1語ずつあります。

1. 最終戦は日曜日に市営スタジアムで行われる。

The (　　　　　) (　　　　　) will (＿＿＿＿＿) (　　　　　) on
(　　　　　) at the (　　　　　) (　　　　　).

place	game	stadium	Sunday	municipal	part	final	take

2. 大丈夫だよ。すべてうまくいくよ。私のことばを信じていいよ。

You'll be (　　　　　) (　　　　　). Everything will be (＿＿＿＿＿)
(＿＿＿＿＿) of. (　　　　　) have (　　　　　) (　　　　　).

care	all	taken	my	looked	right	word	you

3. 国際試合が終わると、日本の観客はよく、自分たちの席のあたりを掃除する。

(　　　　　) (　　　　　) international games, Japanese (　　　　　)
often (＿＿＿＿＿) (　　　　　) the (　　　　　) (　　　　　) their
seats.

attending	areas	around	cleaning	spectators	clean	after	up

4. その学生は試験中にカンニングが見つかって停学になった。それが彼への教訓となった。

The student was (　　　　　) (　　　　　) (　　　　　) an exam and was
(　　　　　) (　　　　　) school. That (＿＿＿＿＿) him a (＿＿＿＿＿).

taught	caught	from	participated	lesson	cheating	during	suspended

1. What can people do to save the ocean for future generations?

2. What pets do you like the best? Why? If you don't have pets, why not?

UNIT 10

"Robot Cafe" Showcases AI's Potential

自販機で示す AI の可能性

'ROBOT CAFÉ' SHOWCASES AI'S POTENTIAL

スマホアプリを使って注文すると、コーヒーが完全自動で提供されるAIカフェロボットが話題である。このビジネスの創業に関わったのは若くしてCEOに就いた中尾渓人さんで、その自販機は最近都内のビルなどで見かけるようになった。今回NHKワールドはAIロボットと労働者の関係などビジネスのあり方について彼の意見を聞いた。

放送日 2022/4/21

Words & Phrases

CD 20

以下の単語や熟語の音声を聞きながら発音に注意し、意味を確認しましょう。

☐ to **showcase** 　　〜を紹介する、出し物にする

例文 This bar in Shibuya *showcases* a young jazz pianist.
　　この渋谷のバーは若手のジャズピアニストを売りにしている。

☐ to **brew** 　　〈コーヒーなど〉を淹（い）れる、作る
☐ **app** 　　アプリ
☐ **aroma** 　　香り
☐ **cup of joe** 　　《口語》1杯のコーヒー
☐ **CEO** 　　最高経営責任者
☐ **home appliances** 　　家電
☐ **precision** 　　正確さ、精度
☐ **fulfilling** 　　満足のいく
☐ **passion** 　　情熱、熱意
☐ to **launch** 　　〜を立ち上げる、〜に着手する

例文 The prime minister finally *launched* his new program of social reforms.
　　首相はようやく社会改革の新しい企画に乗り出した。

以下は、家電などに関する語彙です。下の空所に適切な単語を記入しましょう。

例	家電	(**home**) **appliances**
1.	掃除機	(**v**) cleaner
2.	炊飯器	( ) cooker
3.	冷蔵庫	(**re**)
4.	冷凍庫	(**f**)
5.	洗濯機	(**w**) machine
6.	エアコン	air (**c**)
7.	ノートパソコン	(**la**) computer
8.	(ジュースなどを作る)ミキサー	(**bl**)
9.	電気スタンド	(**d**) lamp / floor lamp
10.	ミシン	(**se**) machine
11.	扇風機	electric (**f**)
12.	電子レンジ	(**mi**) oven
13.	自販機	(**v**) machine
14.	除湿器	(**de**)

1st Viewing >> **Watch the News**

ニュースを見て、内容と合っているものは T 、違っているものは F を選びましょう。

1. Some of the coffee beans used by this cafe robot come from Costa Rica.　T・F

2. Nakao was interested in home economics during his childhood.　T・F

3. Nakao established his venture business when he was in high school.　T・F

Understand the News

1 ニュースをもう一度見て、各問の空所に入る適切な選択肢を a ~ c から選びましょう。

1. Nakao has joined in _____ since he was in junior high school.

   a. national baseball competitions
   b. international robotic tournaments
   c. local mathematic competitions

2. Nakao wants to have robots _____.

   a. take away people's jobs
   b. help people to improve their lives
   c. compete with people for efficiency

3. Nakao wants to contribute to _____.

   a. sports like soccer in the future
   b. nursery school education
   c. the field of construction as well

2 ニュースに関して、空所に入る適切な数字を枠内から選びましょう。なお、余分な選択肢もあります。

1. Cafe robot users can choose from over ( ) kinds of quality coffee beans.

2. A cup of coffee costs around ( ) dollars.

3. The app for this cafe robot has been downloaded over ( ) times.

4. This CEO is a ( ) -year-old college student.

5. So far, cafe robots have been set up at ( ) different places in Japan.

| 3 | 4 | 5 | 7 | 9 | 18 | 20 | 22 | 23 | 25 | 2,500 | 25,000 | 250,000 |

CDの音声を聞いて、News Story の ❶〜❼ の文中にある空所に適切な単語を書き入れましょう。音声は2回繰り返されます。

Anchor: A young Japanese engineer is using artificial intelligence and robotic technology to improve people's lives. One way he's doing that is with a cafe robot that takes the art of **brewing** coffee to a new level.

5 **Narrator:** This coffee vending machine in Tokyo Shinjuku Station is proving a hit with customers. They use a special **app** to place advance orders.

Woman: I order in the train and pick it up here. It makes me happy.

Man: ❶ The **aroma** is completely different from (¹)

10 (²) (³) (⁴)

(⁵) (⁶) (⁷).

❶ 私がいつも飲む缶コーヒー

Narrator: Customers can choose from more than seven kinds of high-quality beans, from countries like Guatemala and Costa Rica. A cup of freshly brewed coffee costs about four dollars.

15 ❷ (¹) (²) (³)

(⁴) (⁵) (⁶)

(⁷) is artificial intelligence. Users send feedback about the coffee based on its richness, bitterness or aroma. This cafe robot uses AI to recommend beans for

20 the next time they order a **cup of joe**. The app has been downloaded more than 25,000 times.

❷ この自販機をさらに特別なものにしているのは

Twenty-two-year-old university student Nakao Keito is **CEO** of the company that developed the cafe robot.

Nakao Keito (CEO, New Innovations): My dream is to provide zero staff services in

25 all industries.

Narrator: ❸ Nakao has been interested in **home appliances** and

electronics (¹) (²)

(³) (⁴) (⁵)

(⁶). He won the national robot soccer

30 tournament and competed in the world championship when

❸ 自分が子どものときからずっと

he was a junior high school student. People called Nakao "Robot Boy."

Nakao: Robot development is never complete. ❹ It is exciting
(¹) (²) (³)
5   (⁴) (⁵) (⁶).

❹ 永遠にずっと改良し［働き］続けることができるから

Narrator: ❺ Nakao's **passion** to develop robots and software
(¹) (²) (³)
(⁴) (⁵) (⁶).

❺ 〜は彼が成長するにつれて、着実に大きくなった

He **launched** his own company when he was in senior high.
10   Nakao's goal was to develop robots that use AI to perform tasks and services normally done by humans. The idea was to make people's lives easier.

Nakao: Technology allows us to create services featuring a high degree of **precision**. My goal is not to have robots take
15   people's jobs, but to help as many people as possible to lead better and more **fulfilling** lives.

Narrator: These cafe robots have been installed at nine locations across the country. Nakao is shooting for 2,500 eventually. He's also thinking about using AI and robotic technology to tackle labor
20   shortages in fields like construction and nursing care.

Nakao: ❻ I hope to provide value by (¹)
(²) (³) (⁴)
(⁵) (⁶) (⁷)
that we face.

❻ 深刻な社会問題の解決を提供する

25 *Narrator:* Nakao has recently been working with a leading global brand to develop a showcase that doubles as a locker. Customers can pick up items they've ordered without the help of shop clerks. ❼ Nakao believes his AI robots have unlimited potential to transform our lives, (¹)
30   (²) (³) (⁴)
(⁵) (⁶) (⁷).

❼ 単にコーヒー一杯で始まって（いるが）

Note: cafe も café も認められた形であるが、Unit 11の形、cafe に統一する。

各問、選択肢から適切な単語を選び、英文を完成させましょう。なお、余分な単語が1語
ずつあります。

1. このスマホのアプリを使えば、前よりはるかにもっと簡単に写真の整理<u>ができますよ</u>。

    This smartphone (   ) (_____) (   ) to organize
    pictures (   ) (   ) more (   ) than (   ).

before	you	a	allows	an	easily	app	lot

2. 今度の映画では、将来性のある若い俳優が<u>主役になる</u>。

    A (   ) (   ) actor is (   ) to <u>be</u> (_____) in
    the (   ) (   ).

movie	promising	young	goal	upcoming	featured	going

3. このボランティア活動に<u>できるだけ多くの人</u>に参加してほしい。

    I'd like (_____) (   ) people as (_____) to (   )
    (   ) in this volunteer (   ).

part	many	activity	participate	as	take	possible

4. パンデミックがおおかた収まったので、翌年の売り上げ100パーセント増を<u>目標にして</u>いる。

    (   ) the pandemic largely (   ) (   ), we are
    (_____) (_____) a 100% (   ) in (   ) next
    year.

out	sales	with	control	for	increase	shooting	under

1. Would you be interested in using your smartphone to order from this coffee
    machine? Why or why not?

2. Which would you prefer: working for a big established company or a small venture
    business? Why? Explain.

UNIT 11

More Than Just a Cafe

故郷に足湯カフェ

MORE THAN JUST A CAFE

福島市郊外の土湯温泉町に、店内で足湯に浸かりながら食事ができる珍しいカフェがある。店主の二瓶さんはこの町で育ったが、上京してからは退職後も関東地方で暮らしている。東日本大震災時には福島の被害に心を痛めていた。地元愛が強く、週末は遠路、自宅から通ってこの店を営業しており土湯の発展に貢献している。

放送日 2022/1/4

Words & Phrases

CD 22

以下の単語や熟語の音声を聞きながら発音に注意し、意味を確認しましょう。

☐ **scores of** 　　　多くの

例文 I receive *scores of* emails every day.
　　私は毎日多くのメールを受け取る。

☐ **footing** 　　　基礎、基盤

☐ **disaster** 　　　災難

☐ **healing-themed** 　癒しをテーマにした

☐ **footbath** 　　　足湯

☐ to **ache** 　　　痛む

☐ to **plummet** 　　　落ち込む

例文 The baseball player's popularity *plummeted* due to the scandal.
　　スキャンダルのため、その野球選手の人気は地に落ちた。

☐ **inn** 　　　旅館

☐ to **compel** 　　　〈人に無理に〉〜させる

☐ to **take action** 　行動を起こす

☐ **restful** 　　　閑静な

Before You Watch

以下は、温泉やお風呂に関する語彙や表現です。下の枠内から適切な単語を選び、空所に入れましょう。なお、余分な単語もあります。

1. 温泉保養地   (   )

2. 露天風呂   (   ) bath

3. 銭湯   (   ) bath

4. サウナ   (   )

5. 砂風呂   (   ) bath

6. ジェットバス   (   ) bath

7. 入浴剤   bath (   )

8. 疲労回復   recovery from physical (   )

9. 浴槽にお湯を張った。   I (   ) the bathtub.

10. シャワーを浴びた。   I (   ) a shower.

11. 温泉に浸かると健康に多くの効能がある。

    Soaking in hot spring water can (   ) your health.

12. 公衆浴場では湯船で体を洗ってはいけない。

    Don't (   ) your body in the tub of the public bath.

13. 公衆浴場では湯船にタオルを浸してはいけない。

    Don't (   ) your towel in the tub of the public bath.

14. 入れ墨があると入れない温泉がある。

    People with (   ) are often not admitted to hot springs.

benefit	dip	drained	electric	exhaustion	filled
foot	medicated	open-air	powder	public	sand
sauna	spa	tattoos	took	wash	whirlpool

1st Viewing ≫ Watch the News

ニュースを見て、内容と合っているものは T 、違っているものは F を選びましょう。

1. Three times a week, Nihei travels far to his cafe in Fukushima Prefecture.   T・F

2. Many inns in his hometown had to close due to the earthquake.   T・F

3. Nihei had opened the footbath cafe in his childhood home before he retired.   T・F

2nd Viewing >> **Understand the News**

1 ニュースをもう一度見て、各問の空所に入る適切な選択肢を a～c から選びましょう。

1. After Nihei Akira graduated from high school, he worked _____.

   a. on a farm in Fukushima
   b. at a bank in the metropolitan area
   c. in a gift shop in Tsuchiyu Onsen

Nihei Akira
Cafe owner

2. After the earthquake and nuclear disaster struck, a _____ encouraged Nihei to do something for his hometown.

   a. friend
   b. relative
   c. farmer

3. Visitors to this footbath cafe can also enjoy _____.

   a. ramen and a vegetable salad
   b. rice balls and miso soup
   c. curry and fruit juice

2 ニュースをもう一度見て、以下の各情報を物事が起こった順番に並べましょう。

1. A big earthquake occurred in the Tohoku District, which includes Fukushima.

2. Nihei Akira opened a footbath cafe in Tsuchiyu Onsen.

3. Nihei Akira started working at a company in Tokyo.

4. NHK World's Kono Akane interviewed Nihei Akira.

Listen to the News Story

CDの音声を聞いて、News Story の ❶〜❼ の文中にある空所に適切な単語を書き入れましょう。音声は2回繰り返されます。

Anchor: Well, Fukushima Prefecture is famous for its hot spring resorts, which once attracted **scores of** visitors, but many are still struggling to regain their **footing** following the nuclear **disaster**. NHK World's Kono Akane interviews a man who found a way to bring in tourists with his **healing-themed** cafe.

Narrator: Tsuchiyu Onsen, just outside Fukushima City: This cafe in the old hot spring town offers something different.

❶ ([1]) ([2]) ([3])
([4]) ([5]) ([6])
([7]), but also her socks, for a relaxing **footbath**.

❶ お客さんは自分の靴を脱ぐだけではなく…

Man: So warm…

Narrator: Every weekend, Nihei Akira travels three hours from his home near Tokyo to open his cafe. ❷ Nihei's parents
([1]) ([2]) ([3])
([4]) ([5]) ([6]).
After graduating from high school, Nihei worked at a bank in Tokyo. ❸ Then ([1]) ([2])
([3]) ([4]) ([5])
([6]), the Tohoku earthquake, tsunami and nuclear disaster struck.

❷ もともとは土産店をここに開いていた

❸ 彼がちょうど退職しようとしていた時に

His heart **ached** as he heard the number of visitors to the hot spring town of his childhood had suddenly **plummeted**, with traditional **inns** closing one after another. It was a conversation he had with a relative that **compelled** him to **take action**.

Nihei Akira (Cafe owner): They sent me peaches which had been radiation-tested, but said to throw them out if I didn't feel comfortable eating them. ❹ Then ([1]) ([2])
([3]) ([4]) ([5])

❹ 私は状況がいかに重大か気が付いた

(⁶). I had to do something.

Narrator: So upon retirement, he converted his childhood home into his space for casual dining and relaxation. And he was determined to take advantage of the hot spring water that had long been pumped straight from the source into his family home. His free-flowing footbath was born.

❺ He constantly monitors the water to (¹)
(²) (³) (⁴)
(⁵) (⁶).

❺ 完ぺきな温度と質を維持する

The visitors also love the curry, which features a local mascot character, and the one-hundred-percent peach juice from fruit grown in Fukushima.

Nihei: I want visitors to enjoy conversations here. ❻ I want to
(¹) (²) (³)
(⁴) (⁵) (⁶).

❻ 温かいもてなしで場所を提供する

Narrator: ❼ By (¹) (²)
(³) (⁴) (⁵)
(⁶) (⁷), Nihei's cozy and **restful** cafe is helping to carry Tsuchiyu Onsen forward.

❼ 地元の魅力を最大限に利用して

各問、選択肢から適切な単語を選び、英文を完成させましょう。なお、余分な単語が1語ずつあります。

1. 私たちがこの地域に引っ越して来てから、次々と問題が起こっている。

Ever (   ) we (   ) into this neighborhood, (   )
have (   ) occurring (_____) (_____) (_____).

> another   problems   since   after   been   moved   others   one

2. 地域の警察は、自転車レーンに駐車違反する車に対して行動を起こすと決めた。

The (   ) (   ) decided to (_____) (_____)
against (   ) (   ) park in (   ) lanes.

> who   action   local   motor   bike   take   people   police

3. 日本のレストランが捨ててしまう食物の多くはまだ食べられる。

(   ) of the (   ) which (   ) in Japan
(_____) (_____) is (   ) (   ).

> throw   much   still   food   edible   take   restaurants   out

4. 一生懸命勉強して、利用できるすべての学習機会を活用すべきだ。

You should (   ) hard and (_____) (_____) of
(   ) the (   ) opportunities (   ) (   )
you.

> available   work   advantage   to   learning   all   take   use

Discussion Questions

1. Do you like traveling? If so, where would you like to go? Why? If not, why not?

2. Are you interested in this footbath cafe or do you prefer regular baths? Explain.

Heeding the Words of Younger People for a Better Future

若きリーダーと脱炭素

EEDING THE WORDS OF YOUNGER PEOPLE FOR A BETTER FUTURE

(株)ユーグレナは、2005年に微細藻類ユーグレナの大量培養技術の確立に成功したが、それを活用した食品や化粧品、更にバイオ燃料の製造や開発も行ってきた。SDGs重視の考え方を基盤にして、未来を創る作業を加速させるため、若手「最高未来責任者」の3代目として、今回、渡部翠（わたべ みどり）さんの就任を決定した。

放送日 2022/12/7

Words & Phrases

CD 24

以下の単語や熟語の音声を聞きながら発音に注意し、意味を確認しましょう。

☐ to **heed**　　　　　　〜に注意を払う

例文 Some patients won't *heed* their doctors' advice.
　　自分の医師の忠告に耳を傾けようとしない患者もいる。

☐ to **tackle**　　　　　　〜に取り組む

☐ **sustainable development goals**　　SDGs、持続可能な開発目標

☐ **biotech**　　　　　バイオテクノロジー、生物工学

☐ **biofuel**　　　　　バイオ燃料、生物燃料

☐ to **extract**　　　　〜を抽出する

☐ **algae**　　　　　　藻類

☐ **euglena**　　　　《生物》ユーグレナ、ミドリムシ〈原生動物で、葉緑体を持ち光合成を行う〉

☐ **photosynthesis**　　《生化学》光合成

☐ to **take**〈something〉**into account**　　〜を考慮に入れる

☐ **carbon-neutral**　　カーボン・ニュートラルの〈地球温暖化の一因である炭素について、排出量と吸収量を同じにして中立にする考え方〉

☐ **candid**　　　　　率直な、遠慮のない

例文 Hiroya gave his *candid* opinion about the new project.
　　浩也は新しい企画について率直な意見を述べた。

以下は、環境問題に関する表現です。下の枠内から適切な単語を選び、空所に入れましょう。便宜上、すべて小文字にしてあります。

1. 最近の若い人たちは、環境問題に関して意識が高い。
   Today's young people are more (   ) about (   ) issues.

2. 残念なことに、海はプラスチックを捨てる巨大なゴミ捨て場になっている。
   Unfortunately, the oceans have become huge (   ) (   ) for plastic.

3. ポイ捨て禁止。
   No (   ) is (   ) here.

4. 地球温暖化は、部分的に二酸化炭素の排出が原因で起こる。
   (   ) warming is partly caused by emissions of (   ) (   ).

5. 環境汚染を防ぐためにすぐに行動を起こすべきだ。
   We should take immediate action to prevent environmental (   ).

6. フロンガスがオゾン層を破壊する。
   Chlorofluorocarbons destroy the (   ) (   ).

7. 熱中症予防には、水分を十分に摂ることが必要だ。
   It is necessary to drink plenty of water to prevent (   ).

8. 温室効果ガスが気温を上昇させる。
   (   ) gases make temperatures higher.

allowed	carbon	conscious	contamination	dioxide
dumps	environmental	global	greenhouse	heatstroke
layer	littering	ozone	waste	

ニュースを見て、内容と合っているものは T 、違っているものは F を選びましょう。

1. The airplane's biofuel was partly made from euglena. T・F

2. The use of biofuel has very little to do with reducing emissions of CO_2. T・F

3. Watabe Midori, a new CFO, is a first-year student at a senior high school. T・F

〉〉 Understand the News

1️⃣ ニュースをもう一度見て、各問の空所に入る適切な選択肢を a ~ c から選びましょう。

1. The president of Euglena aims to _____.

    a. make our society more carbon-neutral

    b. establish another company by 2050

    c. continue the CFO system for the next 50 years

2. The company wants to _____.

    a. avoid the production of expensive food

    b. increase the price of their plastic containers

    c. cut their use of plastics in half

3. Euglena eliminated _____.

    a. its outdoor metal garbage bins

    b. all the vending machines in the company

    c. plastic waste containers from their offices

2️⃣ 以下はニュースの概要です。空所に適切な単語を書き入れましょう。語頭の文字（群）は与えてあります。

Euglena is a Japanese firm and is one of the world's many companies fighting against (**cl** ¹) change. The firm succeeded in developing a fuel using an (**al** ²) called euglena. In order to hasten their progress in achieving their SDGs or Sustainable (**D** ³) Goals, the company has appointed high school student Watabe Midori as their new "CFO" or "Chief (**F** ⁴) Officer." She plans to help companies in their (**decarbo** ⁵) efforts.

Listen to the News Story

CDの音声を聞いて、News Story の ❶〜❼ の文中にある空所に適切な単語を書き入れましょう。音声は 2 回繰り返されます。

Anchor: Companies around the world have started to **tackle** climate change by setting their own *sub…*, **sustainable development goals**, that is. ❶ One Japanese firm
(¹) (²) (³)
5 (⁴) (⁵) (⁶).
It's begun to reflect the voices of young people in its business operations with the knowledge that the children of today will inherit the world of tomorrow.

❶ 一段階上に進めている

Narrator: ❷ In September, the **biotech** firm Euglena co-organized
10 a sightseeing flight over the Goto Islands in southwestern Japan, (¹) (²)
(³) (⁴) (⁵)
(⁶).

❷ 最新の商品の宣伝を目的としている

❸ The aircraft the tourists were on (¹)
15 (²) (³) (⁴)
(⁵) (⁶). It was running on a **biofuel** made from oil **extracted** from a type of **algae** called **euglena** and recycled cooking oil.

❸ 普通のジェット燃料で飛んでいるのではなかった

During the production process, euglena absorbs carbon dioxide in the air through **photosynthesis**. **Taking this into**
20 **account**, the use of biofuel made from euglena could help reduce emissions of carbon dioxide in total.

Izumo Mitsuru (Founder and President, Euglena): ❹ (¹)
(²) (³) (⁴)
25 (⁵) (⁶) and create a **carbon-neutral** society by 2050.

❹ 私たちは積極的に〜を成し遂げることを狙っています.

Narrator: Euglena's efforts to reach those goals go beyond the laboratory. *Three years ago*, the company began hiring people up to 18 years of age as senior executives. Watabe Midori, a
30 first-year high school student, is the latest.

Watabe: Hi, I am Watabe Midori. Nice to meet you.

Narrator: Her title is CFO, but in this case, it means chief future officer and not chief financial officer. ❺ The

(¹) (²) (³)

(⁴) (⁵) (⁶)

(⁷), and the young executives are paid for their efforts. ❻ Euglena wants the CFOs to **come up with**

(¹) (²) (³)

(⁴) (⁵). Based on a proposal from a previous chief future officer, the company set a target of cutting its use of plastics in half and stopped using plastics for its product containers.

It also got rid of vending machines that sold drinks in plastic bottles and plastic waste bins from its offices. Watabe has just started her turn as CFO but says she intends to pose questions in a **candid** manner to help accelerate decarbonization efforts among businesses and *in* society.

Watabe: I want to be able to help create a state of sustainability that is not limited to climate change and environmental issues, but in every field. ❼ (¹) (²)

(³) (⁴) (⁵)

(⁶) (⁷) as a high school student CFO.

Narrator: The world may appear at times to be racing towards an uncertain environmental future, but with people like Watabe asking tough questions and suggesting changes for the better, there may just be a chance that businesses and indeed society as a whole [*will*] achieve a brighter future that is sustainable and more secure.

❺ 会社は毎年、新しい〜を選びます

❻ 持続可能な、ビジネス戦略に関しての提案」

❼ やれることはすべてやろうと思います

Notes:（p. 70）ℓ. 2　本人が言い直しているように、ここはsustainableの言い間違い

ℓ. 28　2022年放送時点での情報。

（p. 71）ℓ. 16　ここは発音が不明瞭だが、意味的にin が合っている

ℓ. 27　willやcan などの法助動詞が期待されるところ

Review the Key Expressions

各問、選択肢から適切な単語を選び、英文を完成させましょう。なお、余分な単語が1語ずつあります。

1. 新しい政府が今取り組むべき主な問題の一つは、高齢化社会をどうするかである。

(   ) of the (   ) problems the new government should
(_____) now is (   ) to (   ) (   ) an
(   ) society.

> main   with   how   aging   one   rare   tackle   cope

2. 試験前は病気で寝ていた。英語の先生が採点時に、考慮に入れてくれることを願っている。

I was (   ) in (   ) before the exam. I hope my English
teacher will (_____) (   ) (   ) (_____) when
he (   ) my paper.

> into   it   sick   take   account   get   grades   bed

3. ベンチャー企業の社長は社員たちが出費を抑える創造的な解決を思いつくことを望んでいる。

The (   ) of the venture company wants his (   )
to (_____) (   ) (   ) creative solutions to
(   ) on (   ).

> come   with   president   save   up   expenses   employees   to

4. 職場の空間を占める多くのものを処分したいが、仕事で毎年備品がどんどん必要になっている。

I'd like to (_____) (   ) (_____) a lot of the things
(   ) (   ) space in our office, but my job (   ) me
to buy more and more (   ) every year.

> equipment   up   rid   taking   go   requires   of   get

Discussion Questions

1. Explain the good and bad points of changing new CFOs yearly.

2. Who is most responsible for the greatest food loss: homes, stores, others? Explain.

UNIT 13

Wood Would Do

経木（きょうぎ）の文化を守る

天然のアカマツ材で作った経木（きょうぎ）は、抗菌性や通気性に優れ、食品の包装材として以前から存在していた。おにぎりや肉、魚などの包装に良く使われていたが、プラスチックが普及しその価格の安さや強度、汎用性で経木に取って代わった。しかし環境への配慮が重要な現代では経木の良さが再確認されている。

放送日 2022/6/9

Words & Phrases

◎ CD 26

以下の単語や熟語の音声を聞きながら発音に注意し、意味を確認しましょう。

☐ to **replace**　　　　〜に取って代わる

例文 In "Toy Story," Woody said to the old toys, "Hey, listen. No one's going to be *replaced*."
トイストーリーの中でウッディーは古いおもちゃたちに、「誰も捨てられないから（心配しないで）ね」と言った。

☐ **wrapper**　　　　包装材

☐ **red pine**　　　　アカマツ

☐ to **deter**　　　　〜を防ぐ

☐ to **thrive**　　　　繁栄する

☐ **preeminent**　　　卓越した、優れた

☐ to **dwindle**　　　先細りする、少なくなる

例文 Our savings are *dwindling* due to the rise in prices.
物価高のせいで、私たちの貯金は少なくなってきている。

☐ **rectangular**　　　長方形の

☐ **resin**　　　　　　樹脂

☐ **characteristics**　特徴

☐ **trade**　　　　　　（特に手を使う）職業、仕事

☐ **handicraft**　　　手仕事、手細工

☐ to **be wrapped up in**　　〜と密接な関係がある

Before You Watch

以下は、日本の伝統的なものに関する英語表現です。下の枠内から適切な単語を選び、空所に入れましょう。

1. 風鈴　　　　　　　　　wind (　　　　　　　　)

2. 拍子木　　　　　　　　wooden (　　　　　　　　)

3. げた　　　　　　　　　wooden (　　　　　　　　)

4. 天ぷら　　　　　　　　(　　　　　　　　) seafood and vegetables

5. 梅干し　　　　　　　　pickled (　　　　　　　　)

6. 豆腐　　　　　　　　　bean (　　　　　　　　)

7. 納豆　　　　　　　　　(　　　　　　　　) soybeans

8. そば　　　　　　　　　(　　　　　　　　) noodles

9. 醬油団子　　　　　　　soy sauce (　　　　　　　　)

10. もち　　　　　　　　　rice (　　　　　　　　)

11. ソフトクリーム　　　　soft-serve (　　　　　　　　) cream

12. かき氷　　　　　　　　(　　　　　　　　) ice

13. 華道　　　　　　　　　flower (　　　　　　　　)

14. 茶道　　　　　　　　　tea (　　　　　　　　)

15. 武道　　　　　　　　　(　　　　　　　　) arts

arrangement	buckwheat	cake	ceremony	chime	clappers
curd	deep-fried	dumpling	fermented	ice	martial
	plum	sandals	shaved		

1st Viewing >> Watch the News

ニュースを見て、内容と合っているものは T 、違っているものは F を選びましょう。

1. There are a few kyogi manufacturing companies in Nasushiobara. 　T・F

2. Shimakura Hiroaki takes pictures of plastic waste in a city dump. 　T・F

3. The city is interested in using kyogi as a food wrapper. 　T・F

Understand the News

1 ニュースをもう一度見て、各問の空所に入る適切な選択肢を a～c から選びましょう。

Shimakura Akihide

1. Shimakura Akihide's family has been manufacturing kyogi for _____ years.

   a. 17
   b. 50
   c. 70

Shimakura Hiroaki

2. Shimakura Hiroaki used to work at a _____.

   a. tourist association
   b. plastic manufacturing company
   c. photo processing firm

3. Shimakura Hiroaki introduces the _____ online.

   a. process of manufacturing kyogi
   b. method of making bookmarks out of red pine
   c. production of kyogi bento boxes

2 以下はニュースの概要です。空所に適切な単語を書き入れましょう。語頭の文字（群）は与えてあります。

Kyogi is a food (**wr** [1]) made from natural red (**p** [2]) wood, and has excellent antibacterial properties. It has long been used as a packaging material for food like (**r** [3]) balls. But (**pl** [4])《複数形》 have taken the place of wood because of their strength and versatility. In Nasushiobara, the Shimakura factory is now the only company which (**manu** [5]) kyogi. However, in today's world, where consideration for the (**env** [6]) is important, kyogi is making a comeback.

Listen to the News Story

CDの音声を聞いて、News Story の ❶〜❼ の文中にある空所に適切な単語を書き入れましょう。音声は2回繰り返されます。

Anchor: Plastics in Japan have **replaced** a thinly-sliced wood as a food **wrapper** called kyogi, but today the conventional, eco-friendly approach is making a comeback.

Narrator: When you buy an onigiri rice ball from this shop, you get it
5　　　　packaged in Japanese **red pine**.

Saito Mami: ❶ (¹) (²) (³)
　　　　(⁴) (⁵) (⁶)
　　　　(⁷), so it's ideal for onigiri.

　　　　❶ 木は見た目もいいし、湿り気も維持する

Narrator: ❷ (¹) (²) (³)
10　　　(⁴) (⁵) (⁶)
　　　　(⁷), and it's said to **deter** bacteria. The city of Nasushiobara used to have a **thriving** kyogi industry, based on wood from the area. However, plastics became **preeminent**, and the number of kyogi manufacturers
15　　　**dwindled**. Only one such company remains in the city.

　　　　❷ 経木は紙のように薄く削られる

Shimakura Akihide's family has been in the business for 70 years. ❸ Shimakura uses a machine that's been on the job
(¹) (²) (³)
(⁴) (⁵) (⁶).
20　　　It turns **rectangular** lumber into thin slices of kyogi.
Adjustments are made to match the hardness of the wood and the amount of **resin**.

　　　　❸ 半世紀以上にわたって

Shimakura Akihide: Even trees of the same type have differences. I keep their **characteristics** in mind as I slice them.

25　**Narrator:** Shimakura's son Hiroaki is learning the **trade**.

Shimakura Hiroaki: ❹ I've (¹) (²)
　　　　(³) (⁴) (⁵)
　　　　(⁶) (⁷) yet.

　　　　❹ 父の腕前に達していない

Narrator: Hiroaki used to work with **handicrafts** at the tourism
30　　　association. He's come to realize the importance of kyogi to

76

the community.

Shimakura Hiroaki: The product our family business turns out is valuable.

❺ I'd like to (¹) (²)
(³) (⁴) (⁵)
(⁶) (⁷) too.

Narrator: Hiroaki takes photos of the manufacturing process and posts them online, a visual introduction to kyogi. Recently, the city expressed interest in using kyogi to reduce plastic waste.

❻ Nasushiobara happens to (¹)
(²) (³) (⁴)
(⁵) (⁶) this year. The bento boxes at the event will make use of kyogi.

Shimakura Hiroaki: I'm glad our kyogi is becoming well-known and accepted. ❼ I hope (¹) (²)
(³) (⁴) (⁵)
(⁶) for many years.

Narrator: The technique and material may **be wrapped up in** the past, but kyogi is being repackaged for an environmentally-friendly future.

❺ 将来の世代がそれを楽しめるのを確かめる

❻ 国体を主催する

❼ 私たちはその勢いを維持できる

Review the Key Expressions

各問、選択肢から適切な単語を選び、英文を完成させましょう。なお、余分な単語が1語ずつあります。

1. その投手がすぐに（治って）戻って来ることを願っているが、彼の負ったようなけがは相当な医療が必要となるだろう。

   I (　　　　　　) the pitcher (＿＿＿＿＿＿) a quick (＿＿＿＿＿＿), but an
   (　　　　　　) like (　　　　　　) will require serious (　　　　　　) care.

medical	his	makes	hope	exit	injury	comeback

2. その交通事故の新聞記事は間違っているかもしれない、ということを覚えておいてください。

   (＿＿＿＿＿) (　　　　　　) (＿＿＿＿＿) that the newspaper (　　　　　　)
   about the (　　　　) accident (　　　　) be (　　　　).

wrong	perhaps	keep	article	could	in	traffic	mind

3. ジョージには何年も会ってないけど、彼から（たまたま）連絡があったら知らせてほしい。

   I haven't (　　　　　) George (　　　　　) (　　　　　). If you
   (＿＿＿＿＿) to (　　　　　) from him, please (　　　　　) me
   (　　　　　).

hear	seen	in	let	years	happen	heard	know

4. 私たちの大学にはいくつかの体育館がある。それらの施設を十分に利用してほしい。

   Our university has (　　　　　) (　　　　　). I hope you will (＿＿＿＿＿)
   (　　　　　) (＿＿＿＿＿) (　　　　　) those (　　　　　).

full	several	of	give	use	gyms	make	facilities

Discussion Questions

1. Many restaurants have started using environmentally-friendly materials, such as wooden spoons and paper straws. What do you think of this idea? Why?

2. Kyogi or wood shaving is also used for bookmarks and coasters. What are some advantages and disadvantages of using kyogi for these products?

UNIT 14

Bon Appétit! Ekiben

駅弁文化を海外へ

ON APPETIT! EKIBEN

パリの主要鉄道駅のひとつリヨン駅に期間限定で、鶏めしの駅弁屋がオープンした。鶏めし弁当は秋田で販売されている人気駅弁で、長年伝統的な味を守っている。フランスは浮世絵や相撲、アニメなど日本文化が浸透している国だが、鶏めしは駅弁文化のないフランスでも受け入れられるかどうかが注目される。

放送日 2022/1/11

Words & Phrases

CD 28

以下の単語や熟語の音声を聞きながら発音に注意し、意味を確認しましょう。

☐ **Bon appétit** たくさん召しあがれ〈フランス語、I wish you a hearty appetite.〉
☐ **pandemic** 世界的流行病
☐ **Garr de Lyon** リヨン駅〈パリにある鉄道駅〉
☐ **pop-up shop** ポップアップショップ、出店、一時的な貸店舗
☐ **ToriMéshi** 鶏めし
☐ to **delight** 非常に喜ぶ、楽しむ
☐ **bid** 入札
☐ **thanks to** 〜のおかげで
☐ **decade** 10年〈dec(a)- は 10 を表す〉
☐ to **take off** 売れ行きがいい

例文 Now that COVID is under control, the economy is *taking off* again.
コロナ感染がコントロールできるようになった今、景気がまた上向きになりかけている。

☐ **signature** 特徴的な、代表的な

例文 "Imagine" became John Lennon's *signature* song in later years.
イマジンは後年、ジョン・レノンの代表的な曲になった。

☐ to **feature** 〜を宣伝する
☐ to **envision** 〈未来のこと〉を想像する、を夢見る
☐ **taste buds** 味覚芽

以下は、秋田県に関係する事柄の説明です。下の枠内から適切な単語を選び、空所に入れましょう。なお、選択肢には余分な単語もありすべて小文字で表記してあります。

1. The Akita Kanto (　　　　　　　　) is celebrated annually during the summer in Akita City. In the parade, performers carry 5- to 12-meter-long bamboo poles while balancing 24 or 46 lanterns on their (　　　　　　　　), foreheads or shoulders. The parade is held in hopes of a good (　　　　　　　　).

2. The Namahage are ogre-like beings and are considered to be (　　　　　　　　) of the gods during a New Year's ritual held on the Oga Peninsula of Akita Prefecture. Performers pretending to be Namahage wear scary (　　　　　　　　) and straw capes, and visit people's homes, scolding children who are lazy or who (　　　　　　　　) badly.

3. Shirakami Sanchi (or Shirakami Mountain Range) is Japan's first World (　　　　　　　　) Site and is located in the area between Akita and Aomori Prefectures. It has a natural beech (or *buna*) forest (　　　　　　　　) by modern civilization. This is one of the largest beech forests in the (　　　　　　　　).

4. Hachi was the name of a dog famous for being (　　　　　　　　). He was an Akita Inu, a Japanese breed of dog (　　　　　　　　) to Akita Prefecture. For nine years, he waited at the train station for his (　　　　　　　　) who had died. His bronze statue sits in front of Shibuya Station. Hachi is the most famous Akita Inu in Japan. Two movies about his life have been made, one in Tokyo and one in Hollywood.

5. Suga Yoshihide served as Prime Minister [PM] of Japan from 2020 to 2021. He was born in Akita Prefecture in 1948. The Second Tokyo (　　　　　　　　) were held when he was the PM. Before becoming PM, he successfully served as Chief Cabinet Secretary from 2012 to 2020 during the second (　　　　　　　　) of PM Abe Shinzo.

administration	behave	festival	harvest	heritage	loyal
masks	master	messengers	native	olympics	
only	palms	triple	untouched	world	

1st Viewing ≫ **Watch the News**

ニュースを見て、内容と合っているものは T 、違っているものは F を選びましょう。

1. Rice grown in Akita Prefecture is used for these ekiben lunch boxes.　　T・F

2. The pop-up shop had to be closed for a while because of the pandemic.　　T・F

3. This pop-up ekiben shop will become a regular shop in the near future.　　T・F

1 ニュースをもう一度見て、各問の空所に入る適切な選択肢を a ~ c から選びましょう。

1. Akita's ToriMéshi has been sold in Japan for _____.

 a. around 50 years
 b. three quarters of a century
 c. over ten decades

2. In this pop-up shop at a main station in Paris, _____.

 a. a vegetarian bento is being sold
 b. three kinds of bento are on sale
 c. soba noodles will soon be available

3. The bento menu introduced in this news was designed by _____ in Akita.

 a. some elementary school students
 b. a group of high school students
 c. a professional Japanese chef

2 右の文字列を並べ替えて単語を作り、各文の空所に入れて意味がとおるようにしましょう。

1. Ekiben is a Japanese lunch box that train riders eat during their (**jo**   )《複数形》.   [eunrys]

2. "Bon (   )" is an expression in French, said to someone before he/she starts eating a meal.   [taptipé]

3. In 2019, a Japanese (   ) shop, which sold chicken lunch boxes, was opened in Paris.   [pppuo-]

4. COVID-19 caused a recent (**p**   ) which spread all over the world.   [emandic]

CDの音声を聞いて、News Story の ❶～❼ の文中にある空所に適切な単語を書き入れましょう。音声は 2 回繰り返されます。

Anchor: A company from northern Japan that makes ekiben, or box lunches sold at train stations, is getting to experience the dream of a lifetime, despite the **pandemic**.

❶ The firm's travel-friendly products have gone on sale

(¹) (²) (³)

(⁴) (⁵) (⁶)

(⁷) in Paris. NHK World's Isojima Ryo has the story.

❶ もっともにぎやかな駅のひとつで

Narrator: The **Garr de Lyon** in Paris. The major train terminal connects to many other European countries. Last year, a Japanese company opened a unique **pop-up shop** here, selling its specialty, ekiben from Odate Station in Akita Prefecture.

Prize Akita rice, steamed in a soy-sauce-seasoned broth, is topped with savory sweetish chicken. **ToriMéshi** has been an Akita delicacy for 75 years. ❷ (¹)

(²) (³) (⁴)

(⁵) (⁶).

❷ 弁当は人気がある

❸ In Japan, travelers **delight** in choosing ekiben at stations

(¹) (²) (³)

(⁴) (⁵) (⁶).

❹ (¹) (²) (³)

(⁴) (⁵) (⁶),

the company targeted the country as a place to start promoting both ekiben culture and Akita flavors abroad.

❸ 電車での旅で食べるために

❹ フランスの広範囲にわたる鉄道網のために

In 2019, the company opened a small shop in Paris as its first step. Although it was forced to close for some time due to the pandemic, later its sales more than doubled, **thanks to** demand for takeaway. Eventually, the company won its **bid** to open a shop in the Garr de Lyon.

82

Yagihashi Shuichi (Resident, Hanazen): ❺ I think ekiben is a form of Japanese

fast food (¹) (²)

(³) (⁴) (⁵)

(⁶). I hope that it **takes off** in France as

well.

Narrator: The store sells six types of ekiben, including its **signature**,

ToriMéshi, as well as vegetarian sushi. These days the Akita

bento, **featuring** regional specialties, is selling well.

❻ (¹) (²) (³)

(⁴) (⁵) (⁶)

(⁷) with regional motifs created by Akita

elementary school students. This menu was designed by high

school students.

❼ The company president is hoping to motivate young

Akita residents (¹) (²)

(³) (⁴) (⁵)

(⁶) (⁷).

The station pop-up shop runs until May. The company plans

to continue developing the overseas market while satisfying

the **taste buds** of hungry travelers. Isojima Ryo, NHK World.

❺ 何十年も伝わって
きた

❻ 弁当を買い求めた
お客さんはキーホ
ルダーがもらえる

❼ 世界を自分たちの
舞台と考えること

Review the Key Expressions

各問、選択肢から適切な単語を選び、英文を完成させましょう。なお、余分な単語が1語ずつあります。

1. テイラー・スウィフトのコンサートチケットは、いつも発売と同時に売り切れる。

   The tickets for Taylor Swift concerts (　　　　　) (　　　　　)
   (　　　　　) as (　　　　　) as they (＿＿＿＿＿) (＿＿＿＿＿)
   (＿＿＿＿＿).

sell	go	always	out	buy	sale	on	soon

2. 大雨のため、野球の試合は明後日に延期された。

   (＿＿＿＿＿) (＿＿＿＿＿) the (　　　　　) rain, the (　　　　　)
   (　　　　　) was (　　　　　) until the (　　　　　) after tomorrow.

day	fall	to	postponed	heavy	game	due	ball

3. 皆さんのおかげで、私はここで一緒に働いた年月に多くのことを学びました。

   (＿＿＿＿＿) (＿＿＿＿＿) (　　　　　) of you, I learned (　　　　　)
   (　　　　　) in the (　　　　　) I worked (　　　　　).

here	all	to	many	so	much	years	thanks

4. SNSは私たちの生活に大きな影響を与え、有益なものだけでなく有害なものもある。

   (　　　　　) (　　　　　) are having a (　　　　　) (　　　　　) on
   our (　　　　　), which can be (　　　　　) as (＿＿＿＿＿) as beneficial.

media	huge	harmful	effect	social	lives	well	even

Discussion Questions

1. Do you eat ekiben or boxed lunches? If so, what kind of lunches do you like? Why? If not, why not?

2. Which do you prefer: cooking at home or eating out? What are advantages and disadvantages of each? Explain.

UNIT 15

A New, Improved Tree

エリート秋田杉

NEW, IMPROVED TREE

秋田県は日本有数の杉の産地だが、今「エリート秋田杉」が注目されている。成長が早く二酸化炭素の吸収源として人間の健全な環境に貢献すると期待される。更に花粉の飛散量が減るので、花粉症の人には朗報である。政府は杉に限らず、2030年までに林業用の苗木の30%をエリートツリーにする目標を掲げている。

放送日 2022/7/12

Words & Phrases

CD 30

以下の単語や熟語の音声を聞きながら発音に注意し、意味を確認しましょう。

- [ ] cedar 杉
- [ ] to mature 成熟する、大人になる

  例文 By age 16, most girls have *matured* and reached their full height.
  ほとんどの女の子は16歳までに大人になって、背が最も高くなる。

- [ ] lumber 材木
- [ ] downside 不利な面
- [ ] hay fever 花粉症

  例文 I'm looking for a good medicine to relieve my *hay fever* symptoms.
  花粉症(の症状)に効くいい薬を探しています。

- [ ] to cultivate ～を栽培する
- [ ] sapling 若木
- [ ] to halve ～を半分にする
- [ ] carbon dioxide 二酸化炭素〈化学式 CO_2〉
- [ ] carbon neutrality カーボンニュートラル、炭素中立、炭素循環
- [ ] cone 〈裸子植物の〉球果
- [ ] to lessen ～を減らす
- [ ] optimal 最適の
- [ ] to verify 実証する

以下は、健康状態に関する表現です。下の枠内から適切な表現を選び、空所に入れましょう。なお、余分な選択肢もあります。

1. 花粉症がひどい。　　　　　　　I have bad (　　　　　　　).

2. ほこりにアレルギーがある。　I'm allergic to (　　　　　　　).

3. おなかが痛い。　　　　　　　I have a (　　　　　　　).

4. 喉が痛い。　　　　　　　　　I have a (　　　　　　　) throat.

5. 腰が痛い。　　　　　　　　　I have a (　　　　　　　).

6. コロナ接種の後、熱が出た。

　　　　　　　　　I developed a (　　　　　　　) after I got the COVID shot.

7. 下痢をしている。　　　　　　I have (　　　　　　　).

8. 便秘をしている。　　　　　　I'm (　　　　　　　).

9. めまいがする。　　　　　　　I'm (　　　　　　　).

10. 体調がよくない。　　　　　　I'm (　　　　　　　).

11. 寒気がする。　　　　　　　　I have (　　　　　　　).

12. 食欲がない。　　　　　　　　I have no (　　　　　　　).

13. 足首をくじいた。　　　　　　I (　　　　　　　) my ankle.

14. 膝が出血している。　　　　　My knee is (　　　　　　　).

15. 蚊に刺されたところがまだ痒い。　These mosquito bites still (　　　　　　　).

> appetite　　backache　　bleeding　　burnt　　chills
> constipated　　diarrhea　　dizzy　　fever　　hay fever
> hangover　　house dust　　itch　　nauseous　sore
> sprained　　stomachache　　under the weather

ニュースを見て、内容と合っているものは T 、違っているものは F を選びましょう。

1. The "elite cedars" grow twice as fast as the regular cedars.　　　T・F

2. The "elite cedars" produce around one fifth of the pollen of regular cedars.　T・F

3. The "elite cedars" have fewer male cones to scatter pollen.　　　T・F

1 ニュースをもう一度見て、各問の空所に入る適切な選択肢を a ～ c から選びましょう。

1. To develop "elite cedars," experts chose about 50 cedars of the best size and quality from among _____ cedars.

   a. 1,600
   b. 16,000
   c. 160,000

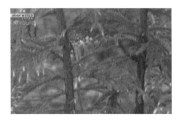

2. Experts are going to test if their cedars will grow in areas with _____.

   a. lots of snow in the winter
   b. quite high summer temperatures
   c. very little rainfall year-round

Sato Hirofumi
Akita Forest Research and Training Center

3. Sato is aiming to create cedars which scatter only _____ of the pollen of standard trees.

   a. 1/10
   b. 1/100
   c. 1/1,000

2 ニュースの二種類の秋田杉に関して、エリート杉（"Elite cedar"）の説明には E、従来の標準的な杉（"Regular cedar"）の説明には R を空所に書き入れましょう。

1. This kind of cedar grows faster. (　　　)

2. This kind of cedar spreads more pollen. (　　　)

3. This kind of cedar absorbs more CO_2. (　　　)

4. Cultivating this kind of cedar can be more expensive. (　　　)

5. This kind of cedar is expected to contribute more to carbon neutrality. (　　　)

Listen to the News Story

CDの音声を聞いて、News Story の ❶〜❼ の文中にある空所に適切な単語を書き入れましょう。音声は2回繰り返されます。

Anchor: Japanese forests are famous for **cedar**. ❶ The trees
(1) (2) (3)
(4) (5) (6).

     But there are **downsides**. Cedars spread a lot of pollen, causing **hay fever**, and **cultivating** them can be expensive. ❷ In our next report, we look at a new breed of cedar that could (1) (2)
(3) (4) (5)
(6).

❶ 成長が早く良い材木になる

❷ より良い林業になる手助けとなる

Narrator: This one-meter-tall **sapling** is a new type of cedar developed in Akita Prefecture, northern Japan. The forestry experts call it an "elite cedar."

Sato Hirofumi (Akita Forest Research and Training Center): Elite cedars grow quickly.

Narrator: This is a regular Akita cedar. ❸ Next to it is an
(1) (2), (3)
(4) (5) (6)
(7).

❸ 同時に植林されたエリート杉である

Sato: These were raised from cuttings the same way, but the growth is very different.

Narrator: Compared with regular Akita cedars, the new trees grow 1 1/2 times faster. As a result, the experts say they can absorb over 1.5 times more **carbon dioxide**.

Sato: The high absorption of CO_2 will help contribute to **carbon neutrality**.

Narrator: Also, because the elite cedars mature quickly, less time and labor *is* needed to maintain plantations. Officials believe this could **halve** the costs.

     There is another reason the experts call their new tree "elite."

Sato: It releases less than half the pollen.

Narrator: The new tree produces very few male **cones**, which scatter

pollen. This could **lessen** the suffering of those who get hay
fever.

❹ The (¹) (²)
(³) (⁴) (⁵)
(⁶) (⁷). Experts in Akita
selected about 50 trees of **optimal** size and quality from
among 16,000 cedars. They took cuttings, planted them,
and monitored their growth and other factors, such as
quantities of pollen-producing cones. ❺ Over two years, they
(¹) (²) (³)
(⁴) (⁵) (⁶).

❻ They are now working to **verify** how well their
cedars grow in snowy regions and (¹)
(²) (³) (⁴)
(⁵) (⁶). If all goes well, they
hope to market the seeds within three years.

Sato: We want to develop varieties of cedar to promote Akita's
             unique qualities for another 50 to 100 years.

Narrator: Sato is not stopping here. One of his goals is to create a
             cedar that produces only one percent of the pollen of a
             standard tree. ❼ The elite cedars of Akita may be good
             news for forestry, (¹) (²),
             (³) (⁴) (⁵)
             (⁶).

❹ エリート杉の開発
は〜年前に開始さ
れた

❺ これらの木のうち
最も良いものを選
択した

❻ どのくらいお金を
節約できるか

❼ 環境（のため）や、
アレルギーに悩ま
されている人のた
めにも

Note: （p. 88）ℓ. 26　文法的には複数形なのだが、口語ではよく単数形になる

各問、選択肢から適切な単語を選び、英文を完成させましょう。なお、余分な単語が 1 語ずつあります。

1. 彼は中学校ロボットサッカーの全国大会で優勝したので、クラスメートは<u>彼</u>を「ロボット少年」<u>と呼んで</u>いた。

   (　　　　　　) he (　　　　　　) the (　　　　　　) robot soccer (　　　　　　)
   in junior high school, his classmates (　　　　　) to (＿＿＿＿＿＿)
   (＿＿＿＿＿＿) "Robot Boy."

tournament	him	won	are	used	because	call	national

2. 現在、家を建てる価格は、10年前<u>と比べて</u>はるかに高い。

   The price of building houses (　　　　　　) is (　　　　　) higher
   (＿＿＿＿＿＿) (＿＿＿＿＿＿) the (　　　　　) (　　　　　) years
   (　　　　　).

ago	compared	today	cost	more	much	with	ten

3. 彼はスキーをしている時ひどい転び方をした。<u>その結果</u> 3 か月松葉杖をついていた。

   He (　　　　　) a (　　　　　) fall (　　　　　) skiing. (＿＿＿＿＿) a
   (＿＿＿＿＿), he was (　　　　　) (　　　　　) for three months.

stretchers	result	nasty	took	as	crutches	while	on

4. 家庭生活より仕事を優先させる<u>人</u>は、退職後よく後悔をすることがある。

   (＿＿＿＿＿) (＿＿＿＿＿) put work (　　　　　) their (　　　　　) life
   often (　　　　　) (　　　　　) after (　　　　　).

it	those	family	employment	retirement	before	regret	who

1. Name someone you know who has allergies like hay fever. What are the symptoms? Explain.

2. Name a famous person you respect who is working hard to protect the environment. What is this person doing? Why do you respect this person?

オンライン映像配信サービス「plus⁺Media」について

本テキストの映像は plus⁺Media ページ（www.kinsei-do.co.jp/plusmedia）から、ストリーミング再生でご利用いただけます。手順は以下に従ってください。

ログイン

ログインページ

- ●ご利用には、ログインが必要です。
  サイトのログインページ（www.kinsei-do.co.jp/plusmedia/login）へ行き、plus⁺Media パスワード（次のページのシールをはがしたあとに印字されている数字とアルファベット）を入力します。

- ●パスワードは各テキストにつき1つです。
  有効期限は、<u>はじめてログインした時点から1年間</u>になります。

[利用方法]

次のページにある QR コード、もしくは plus⁺Media トップページ（www.kinsei-do.co.jp/plusmedia）から該当するテキストを選んで、そのテキストのメインページにジャンプしてください。

メニューページ　　　再生画面

plus+Media トップ　　　メインページ

「Video」「Audio」をタッチすると、それぞれのメニューページにジャンプしますので、そこから該当する項目を選べば、ストリーミングが開始されます。

[推奨環境]

iOS (iPhone, iPad)	OS: iOS 12 以降 ブラウザ：標準ブラウザ	Android	OS: Android 6 以降 ブラウザ：標準ブラウザ、Chrome
PC	OS: Windows 7/8/8.1/10, MacOS X　ブラウザ: Internet Explorer 10/11, Microsoft Edge, Firefox 48以降, Chrome 53以降, Safari		

※最新の推奨環境についてはウェブサイトをご確認ください。
※上記の推奨環境を満たしている場合でも、機種によってはご利用いただけない場合もあります。また、推奨環境は技術動向等により変更される場合があります。予めご了承ください。

本書には音声 CD（別売）があります

NHK NEWSLINE 7
映像で学ぶ NHK 英語ニュースが伝える日本 7

2024年 1 月20日　初版第 1 刷発行
2024年 2 月20日　初版第 2 刷発行

編著者　　山　﨑　達　朗
　　　　　Stella M. Yamazaki
発行者　　福　岡　正　人
発行所　　株式会社　金星堂
（〒101-0051）東京都千代田区神田神保町 3-21
Tel. (03) 3263-3828（営業部）
　　 (03) 3263-3997（編集部）
Fax (03) 3263-0716
https://www.kinsei-do.co.jp

編集担当　稲葉真美香　　　　　　Printed in Japan
印刷所・製本所／大日本印刷株式会社

ISBN978-4-7647-4189-8 C1082

NHK
NEWSLINE

NHK WORLD-JAPAN's flagship hourly news program delivers the latest world news, business and weather, with a focus on Japan and the rest of Asia.

Daily / broadcast on the hour

Journeys in Japan
Explore a different side of Japan. Meet the locals and discover traditions and cultures not usually found in guidebooks!

Tuesdays

ANIME MANGA EXPLOSION
This program will actively feature major "ANIME MANGA" works that are highly recognized by overseas fans and reveal the secrets of Japanese anime and manga creation.

Sundays

GRAND SUMO Highlights
The best of today's sumo! Enjoy daily highlights of this dynamic sport with background info and play-by-play commenta adding to the excitement!

Daily (During tournaments